ONE BLOCK OF WOOD

NINA TOLSTRUP

ONE BLOCK OF
WOOD

15 PROJECTS TO MAKE

PHOTOGRAPHY BY KRISTIN PERERS

COLLINS & BROWN

First published in the United Kingdom in 2010
by
Collins & Brown
10 Southcombe Street
London
W14 0RA

An imprint of Anova Books Company Ltd

Copyright © Collins & Brown 2010

All rights reserved. No part of this publication may be reproduced, stored in a retrieval system, or transmitted in any form or by any means electronic, mechanical, photocopying, recording or otherwise, without the prior written permission of the copyright owner. The patterns contained in this book and the items created from them are for personal use only. Commercial use of either the patterns or items made from them is strictly prohibited.

ISBN 978-1-84340-546-7

A CIP catalogue for this book is available from the British Library.

10 9 8 7 6 5 4 3 2 1

Reproduction by Mission Productions, Hong Kong
Printed and bound by 1010 Printing International Ltd., China

This book can be ordered direct from the publisher at www.anovabooks.com

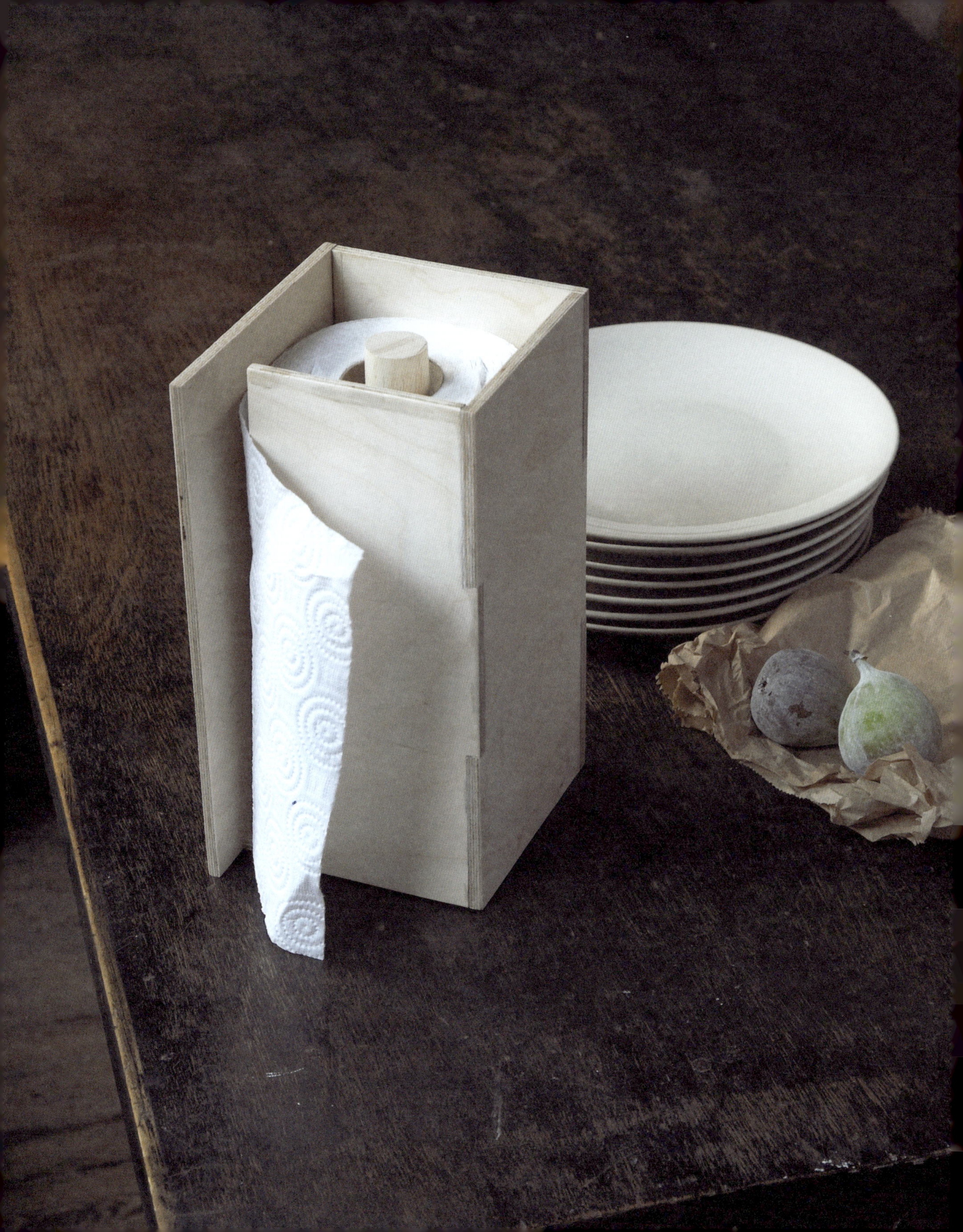

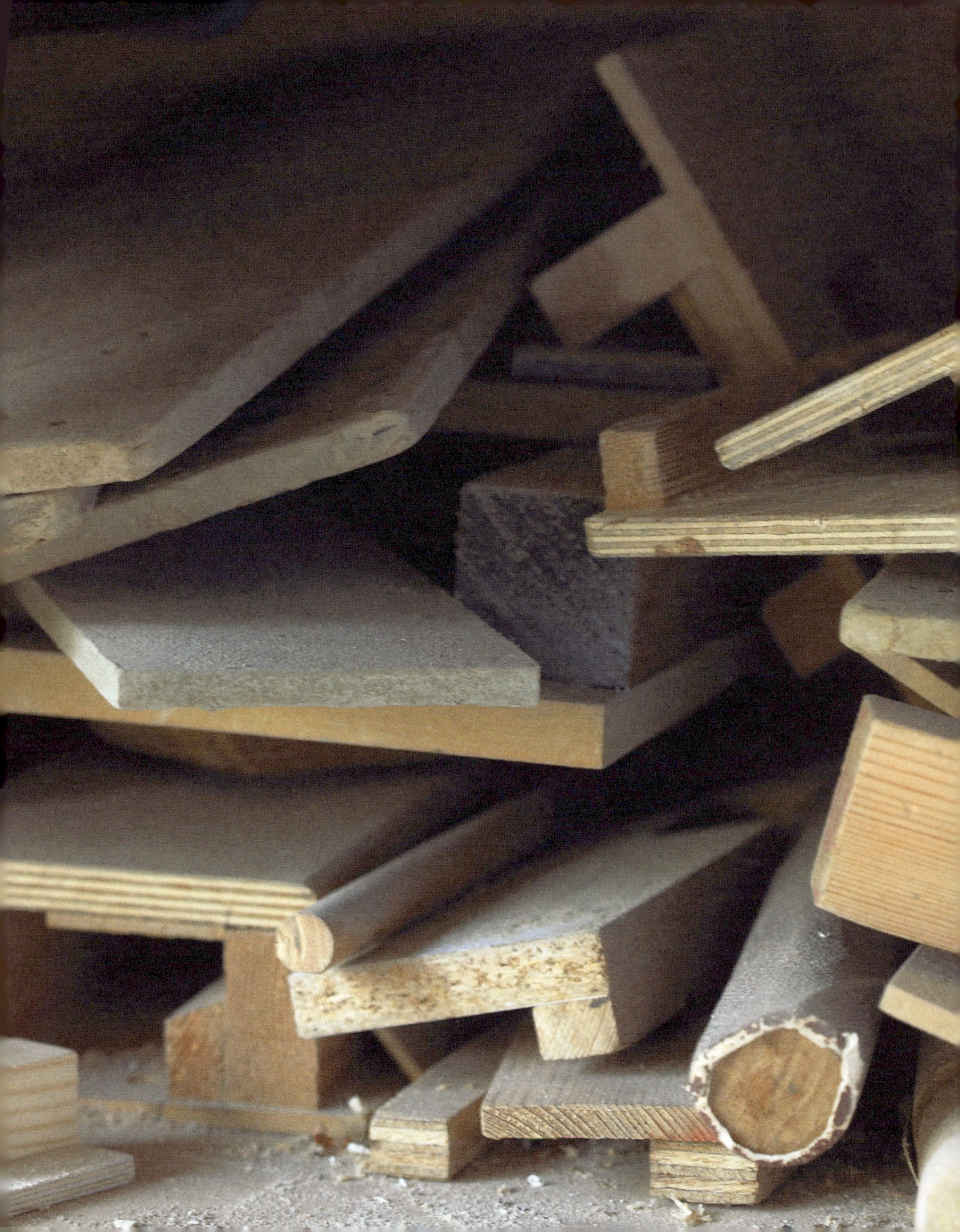

Contents

Introduction	9	Kitchen roll holder	56
The beauty of wood	10	Ruler display	60
Bird feeder	14	Trundle scooter	66
'Nose' hooks	18	Jewellery tree	72
Pallet stool	22	Wonder frames	76
Blackboard robot	28	Twig alphabet	80
Doorstop block	34	Tools and equipment	84
Robot bookends	38	Techniques	92
Elegant trestle	42	Resources	96
Plant holder	46	Acknowledgements	96
Herb carrier	50		

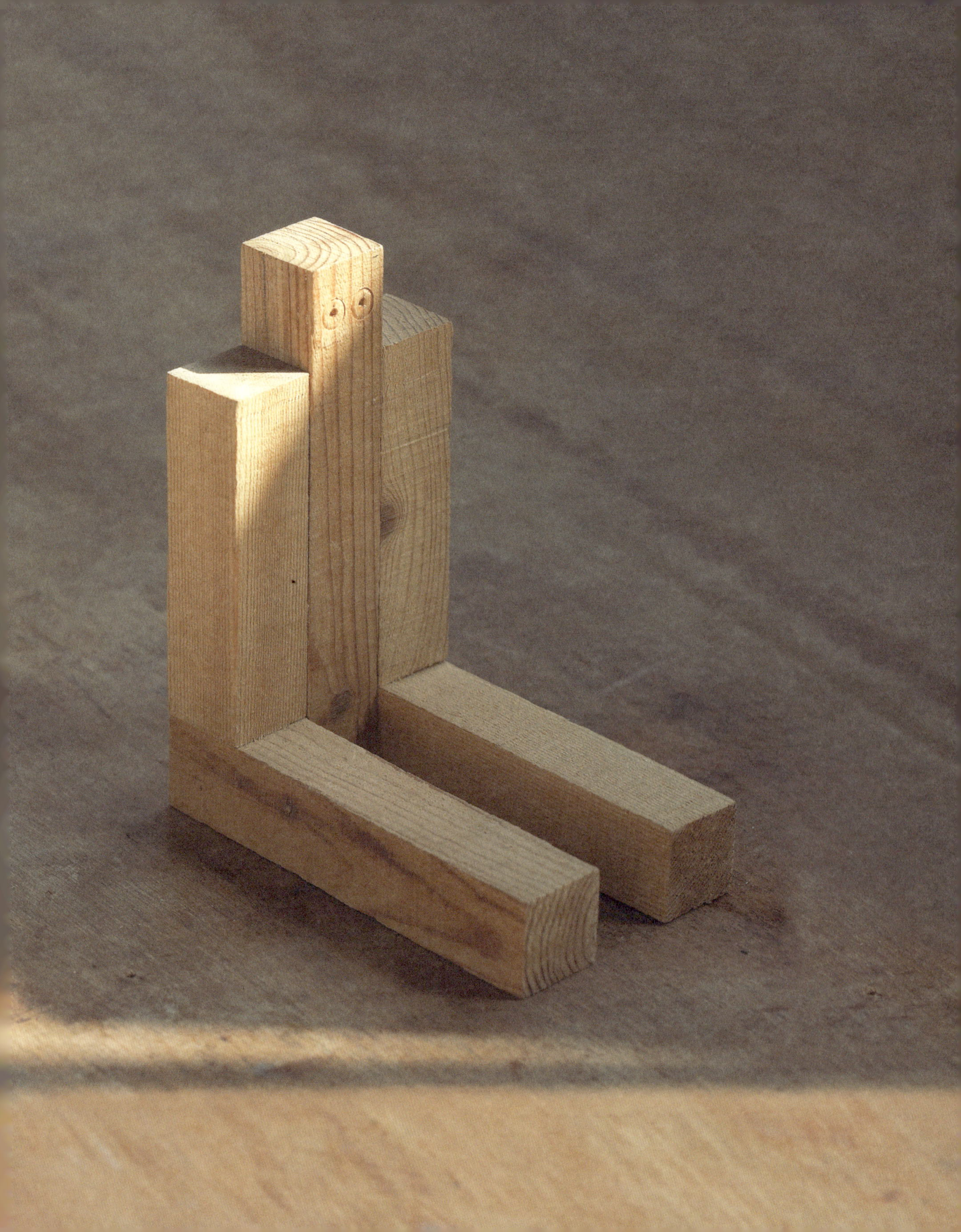

Introduction

The idea behind this book is to provide a source of inspiration for making things in wood. You do not need to have prior woodworking skills – all you need is enthusiasm, patience and a basic toolkit. Give yourself time to enjoy the process of making and revel in the satisfaction of having created something yourself. All the designs can be adapted to fit your tastes and needs, rather like what often happens with a recipe – once you know how to make the dish, you start adding to and changing the ingredients. I hope you will enjoy making some of my designs and maybe even go on to realize your own ideas as you become more confident in the world of the self-made.

Nina Tolstrup

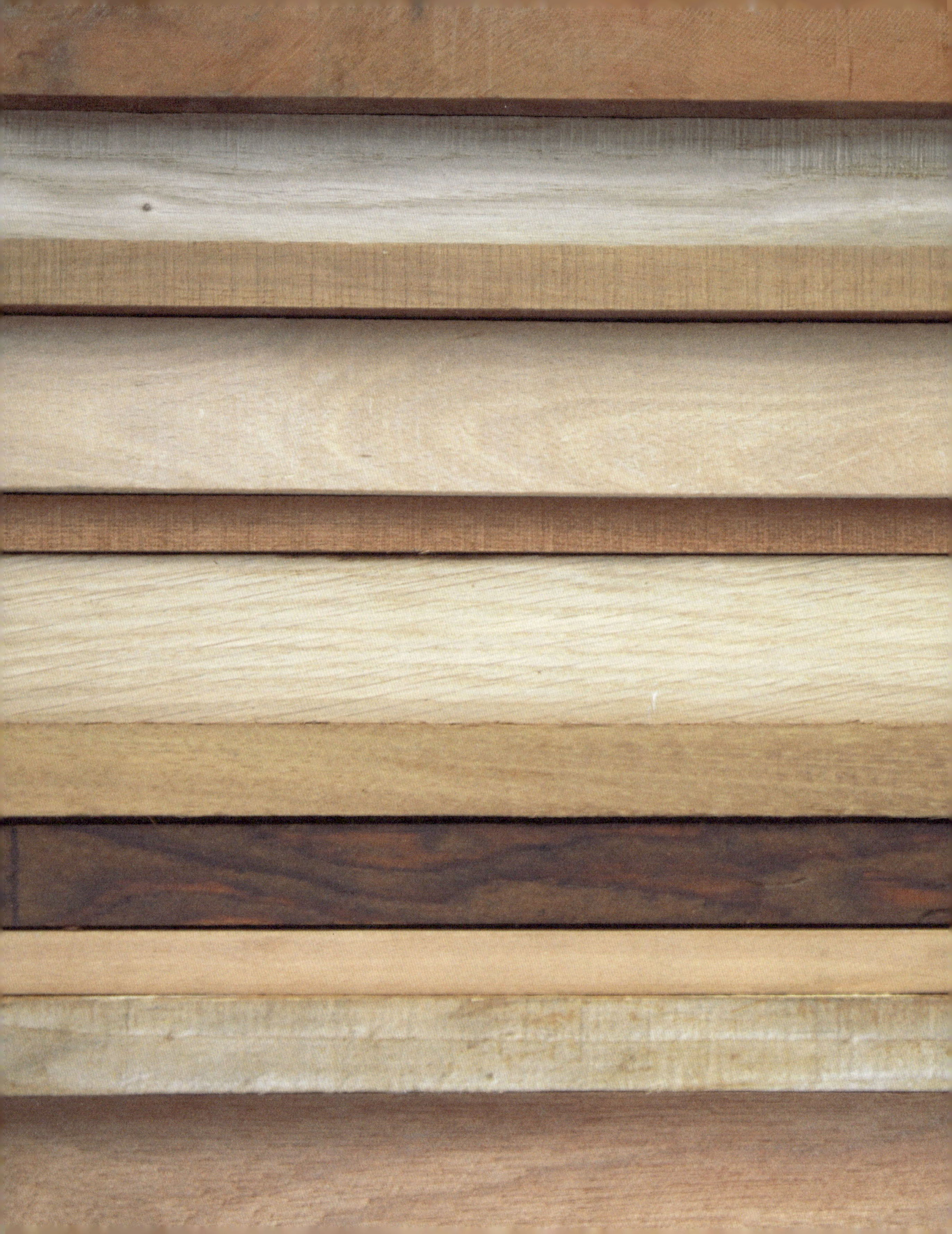

The Beauty of Wood

I love wood. It is the most variable and adaptable raw material. We use it for a wider range of purposes than any other material. Every piece of wood that you handle once served to support a tree's branches and leaves, and to carry sap to nourish them.

As a material, wood is cheaper, warmer, quieter, more resilient and easier to work than stone and metal, and with adequate care, wood mellows to a beautiful patina that adds to the beauty of any wooden object. Timber is plentiful and cheap, it grows naturally, though slowly, and it is a renewable resource. Even though all wood is basically similar, every fragment shows the variability found in natural materials. No two pieces of wood in the world are exactly alike. This gives timber its unique fascination, for no other common durable substance shows patterns and properties peculiar to each piece.

The great Finnish architect, Alvar Aalto, once described wood as a 'form-inspiring, deeply human material'. It is a material that evokes a profound sense of comfort, echoing centuries of domestic use. The wood we use includes a vast range of different species, both hardwoods and softwoods, each with their own special characteristics. Hardwoods such as oak, teak and mahogany have been among the most valued of woods because of their strength, density and resistance to decay. Softwoods are generally much less durable but grow more quickly and are widely used. The term 'wood' today covers many different types of manufactured product, such as plywood, MDF, chipboard and hardboard – these are used in all kinds of building work and furniture-making.

The wood you'll need for the designs in this book doesn't have to be sourced at a timber merchant. I prefer to use recycled wood, if possible, for small projects such as those shown here. Pieces of wood are often left over at the end of building projects, so if any of your neighbours are having work done, they may be able to give you some. Ask a local carpenter – carpenters normally throw out an impressive amount of offcuts and I have found that they are usually happy for you to dig some out of their waste bins. Shopkeepers may be able to help: goods are delivered on wooden pallets and sometimes these are not required for reuse. In some towns there are wood recycling projects where you can purchase wood cheaply. If you do buy wood from a timber merchant, make sure that it is FSC-marked, which guarantees that the wood has come from certified, well-managed, sustainable forests.

THE PLEASURE OF MAKING

In the post-war years, the incentive for DIY was often the saving of money, but today we have got used to being able to buy more or less everything very cheaply and so that no longer applies. Now the incentive for making things yourself is much more likely to be concerned with environmental issues and the pleasure of making. The absorption and satisfaction that creating items in wood provides is life-affirming. You can even enjoy it as a family activity, taking appropriate safety precautions and supervising children at all times. Children who are too young to handle tools can be involved in painting and decorating finished pieces.

Why not make one of the projects as a gift? Some of my most treasured presents are from friends and family members who have made the effort to create something special for me, whether it is a jar of yummy, home-made marmalade, a knitted scarf or a lamp made out of wood from an old box. To give your time seems to me much more valuable than merely spending your money.

If you wish, you can paint the designs. Paints left over after recent household renovations are perfect. Most of us tend to store surplus paints and then end up throwing them all out five years later when we discover they have dried up and are useless.

BUYING WOOD

When you visit a specialist timber merchant, you'll find rough-sawn boards and ready-prepared wood that has been planed and squared on all sides to standard sizes. Its stated size is that of the wood before it is planed; however, it is planed before you buy it, so the actual size is a few millimetres smaller. You can have wood cut to the size you require for a small extra charge.

A wood 'section' is a square or rectangular piece of wood, which is described in terms of its width and thickness; you chop it up into lengths as you require. A dowel, or dowelling, is a round section of wood, which is produced in various diameters. Thick dowelling is sometimes known as broomstick dowelling.

Plywood is a manufactured board made from thin layers of wood glued together, and is available in various qualities. Birch plywood is a top-quality product that is easy to saw and plane to a good finish. This attractive, pale wood has been used for several projects in this book.

MEASUREMENTS

For the projects, use either the metric or imperial measurements, not a mixture of the two systems. The imperial measurements have been adjusted for ease of working and are not an exact conversion of the metric measurements (you may notice that a particular measurement in one system has differing conversions in the other system).

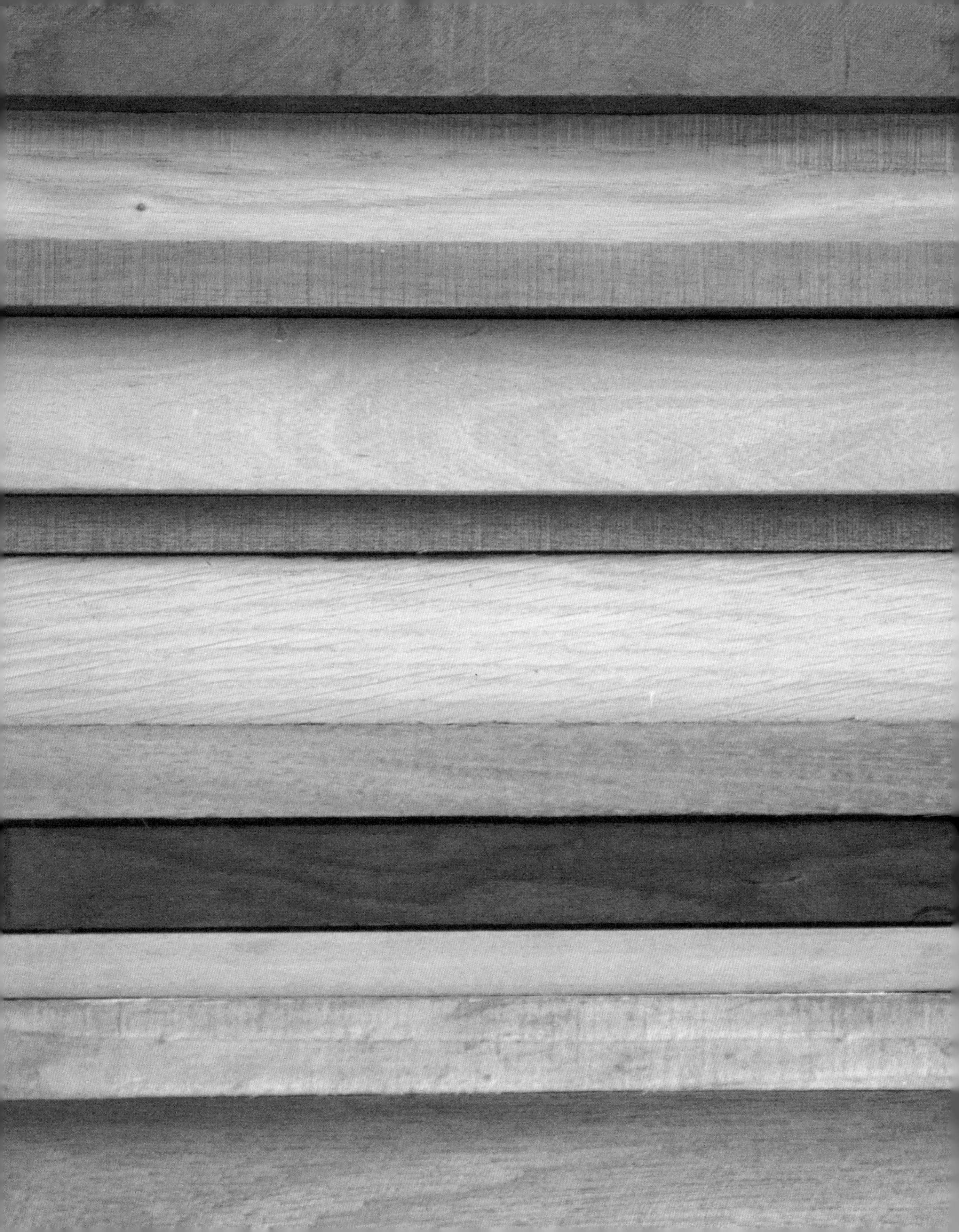

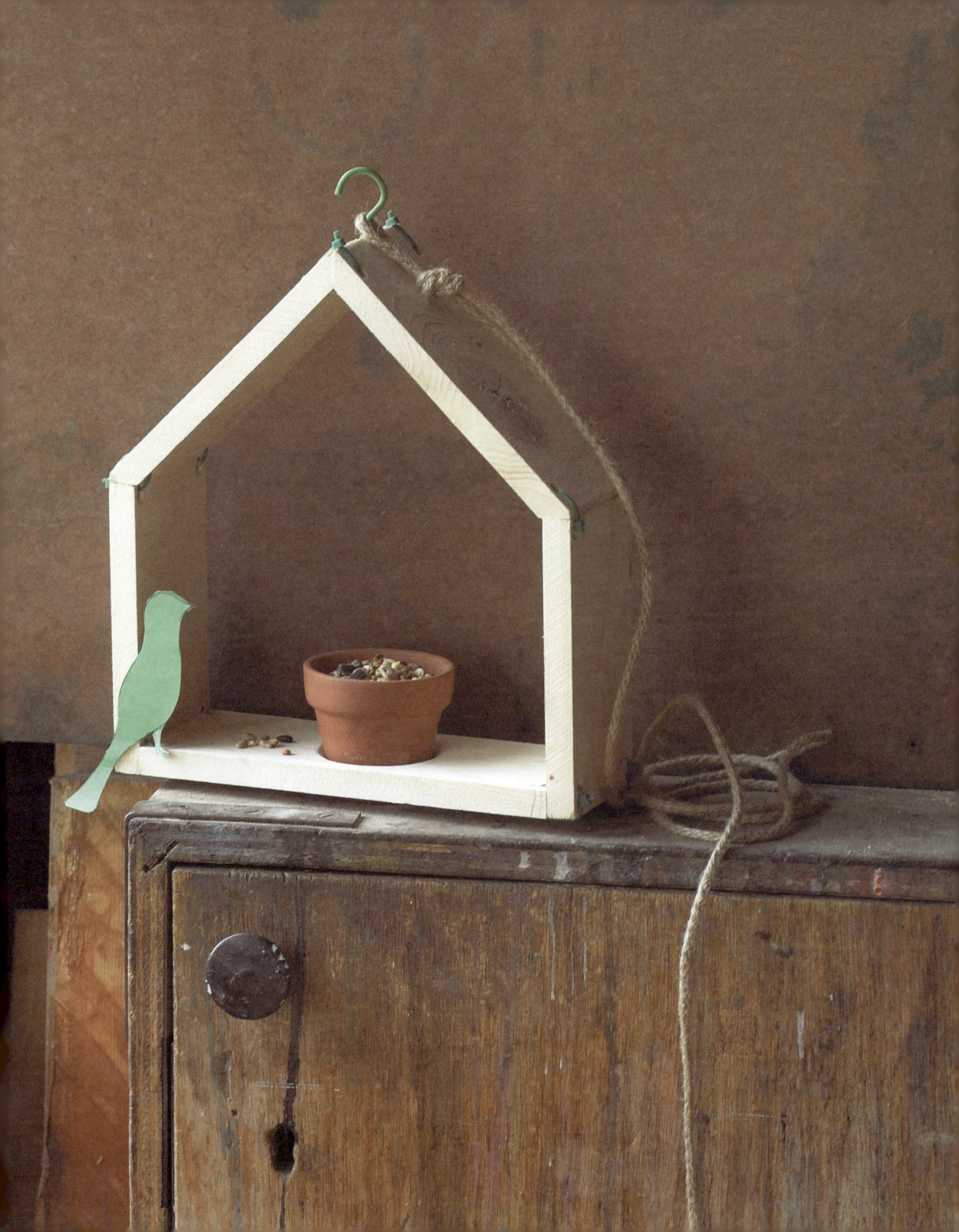

Bird Feeder

The idea behind this bird feeder, which is shaped like a frame, was to create a product that encourages interaction with nature and serves to capture a moment. We are increasingly losing touch with nature as the relentless expansion of cities continues. We rarely seem to catch sight of the little wildlife that we co-exist with. During the winter especially, birds can find it difficult to hunt out sufficient food; by hanging a bird feeder in your garden or on your terrace, you will help local bird life. The frame is held together with cable ties, which are suitable for outdoor use and make it quick and easy to assemble the frame. You can use any kind of found wood or offcuts.

Instructions

WHAT YOU NEED

Wood: 770 x 75 x 12mm (2ft 6in x 3in x 1/2in)
Small terracotta plant pot 70mm (2 3/4in) in diameter at the widest part
Small cable ties: 10 x 2 mm (1/16in) wide
Small hook
Wood glue
Sandpaper (optional)

Saw and mitre box, or electric saw that can cut angles
Drill
Flat drill bit: 3mm
Holesaw: 50mm
Half-round wood file

TECHNIQUES

Measuring and marking: see page 86
Sawing wood: see pages 86-7, 92
Planing and sanding: see pages 87, 92
Drilling holes: see pages 88-9, 92
Gluing and clamping: see pages 93 and 90
Finishes for wood: see page 91
Mitred joints: see page 93

1

Saw up the wood into the following lengths.
Base: 200 x 75mm (8 x 3in)
Sides: two pieces, 130 x 75mm (5 x 3in)
Roof: two pieces, 155 x 75mm (6 x 3in); 45° angle at each end

2

Drill holes for the cable ties that will hold the pieces together, using the 3mm drill bit. Position the holes 15mm (5/8in) in from the top edge of the roof piece and the same distance from the edge on each side of the base. The rest of the holes are 7mm (1/4in) from the edge. Sand all the pieces if you wish.

3

Mark the centre point in the base. Cut a hole to hold the plant pot, using the drill and holesaw. File the inside edge of the hole a little, so the pot will fit nicely in the hole.

4

Put a bit of wood glue on the ends of the pieces and glue them together. The end of the roof piece will overlap the side piece a little as it is cut at an angle. You can cut this off or leave it as it is. Push the cable ties through the holes, join the pieces and tighten the ties.

5

Drill a small pilot hole, centred on the top edge, for the hook. Screw in the hook and tie on a piece of string to hang the bird feeder with. As the bird feeder is to hang outside, it will last longer if painted or stained with wood-preserving paint (make sure that it is wildlife-friendly).

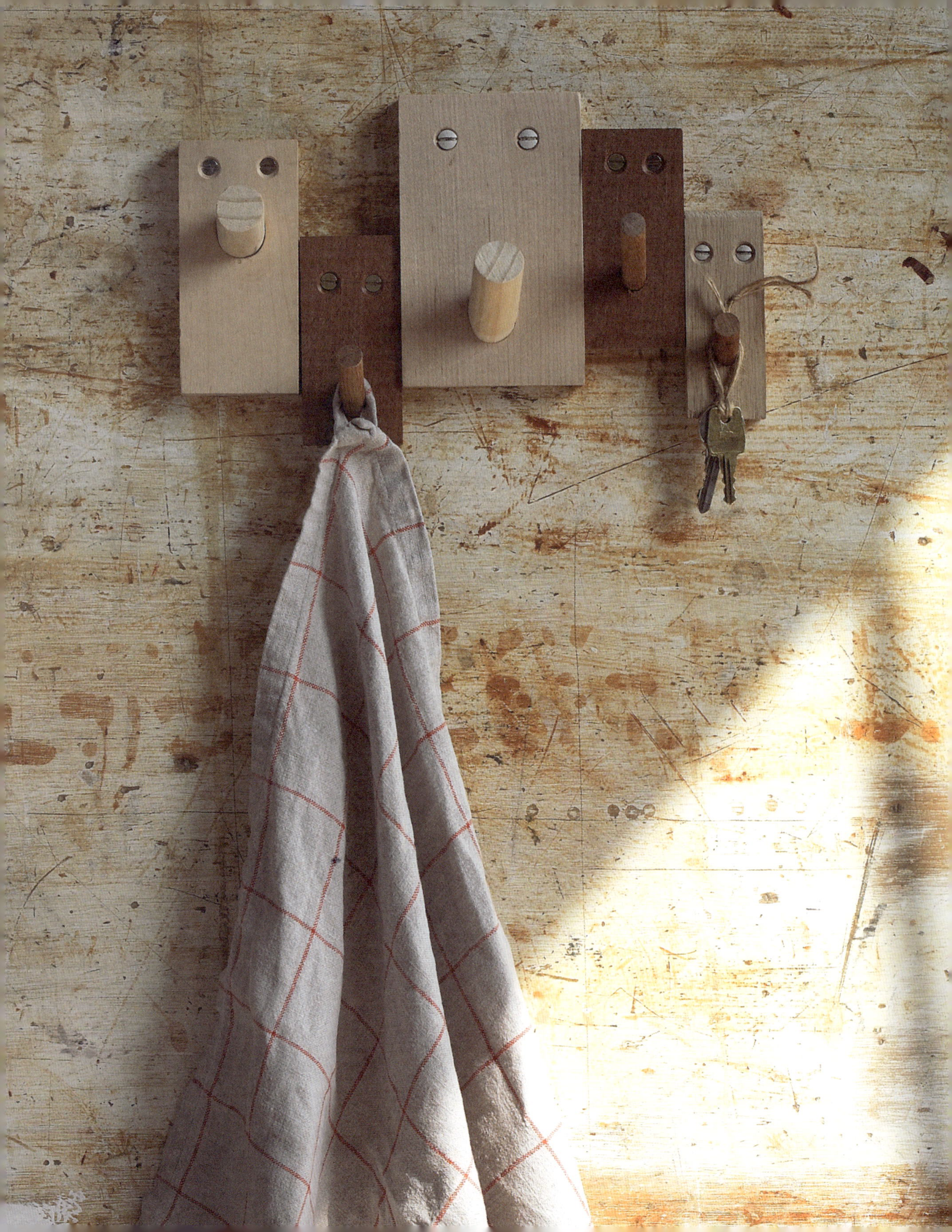

'Nose' Hooks

The 'nose' hook idea came out of the visual impact of two screwholes in a piece of wood, which look like the eyes in a cartoon face. So, adding the nose – long, short, slim or fat – gives the maker the opportunity to create hundreds of different 'nose hook' characters. It is fun to play around with the dimensions and sizes of screws; colour could be added too. The hooks can be used singly, or lined up together to form a coat-hanging wall rack – either in a straight line or offset. Most rectangular offcuts can be used to make the base for the hooks: I have used a variety of oak, cherry and iroko wood.

Instructions

WHAT YOU NEED

For four hooks
Wood (bases):
    120 x 58 x 20mm (5 x 2 x 1in)
    105 x 50 x 18mm (4 x 2 x ¾in)
    140 x 89 x 21mm (5½ x 3 x 1in)
    100 x 38 x 17mm (4 x 1½ x ¾in)
Dowelling: 50–100mm (2–4in) per hook,
    12mm (½in) and 24mm (1in) in diameter
Slot-headed screws, size as required: 8
Wood glue
Sandpaper

Saw
Drill
Pilot-countersink bit: size to match screw size
Flat drill bits: 13mm and 25mm
Screwdriver
Plane

TECHNIQUES

Measuring and marking: see page 86
Sawing wood: see page 86–7, 92
Planing and sanding: see pages 87, 92
Drilling holes: see pages 88–9, 92
Gluing and clamping: see pages 93 and 90

1

Cut the wood for the base pieces. The dimensions given above are just a guide – you can make the rectangles any size you like. Cut four pieces of dowelling for the 'noses'.

20   One Piece of Wood

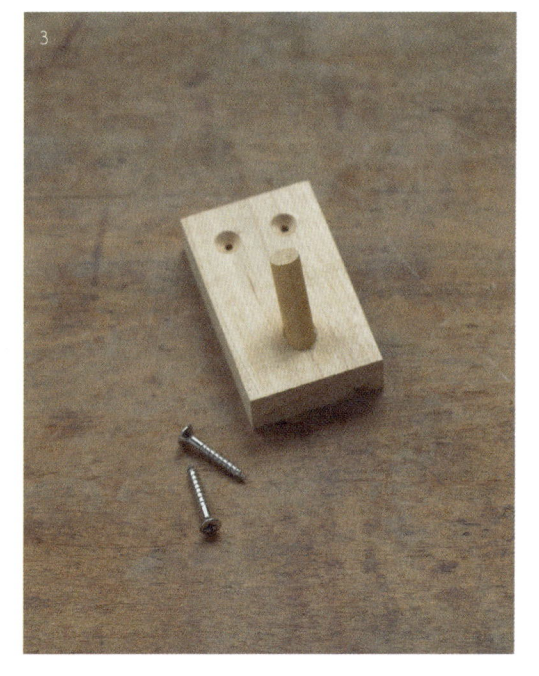

2

Drill two countersunk holes for the screws that form the 'eyes' and which will be used to attach the base to the wall. Space them evenly at the top end of the piece of wood. Drill a hole for the 'nose' in each base, using the appropriate sized drill bit – drill at an angle so that the nose will face upwards.

3

Insert the noses by adding a few drops of wood glue to the hole, then pushing the nose through the hole so that it sticks out a little on the other side of the base.

4

Saw off the end of the 'nose' on the back of the base, then plane until the surface is smooth and flush. Sand all pieces if required.

5

Insert the screws into the countersunk holes (where they become the 'eyes' of the character) and attach the completed 'nose' hook to the wall.

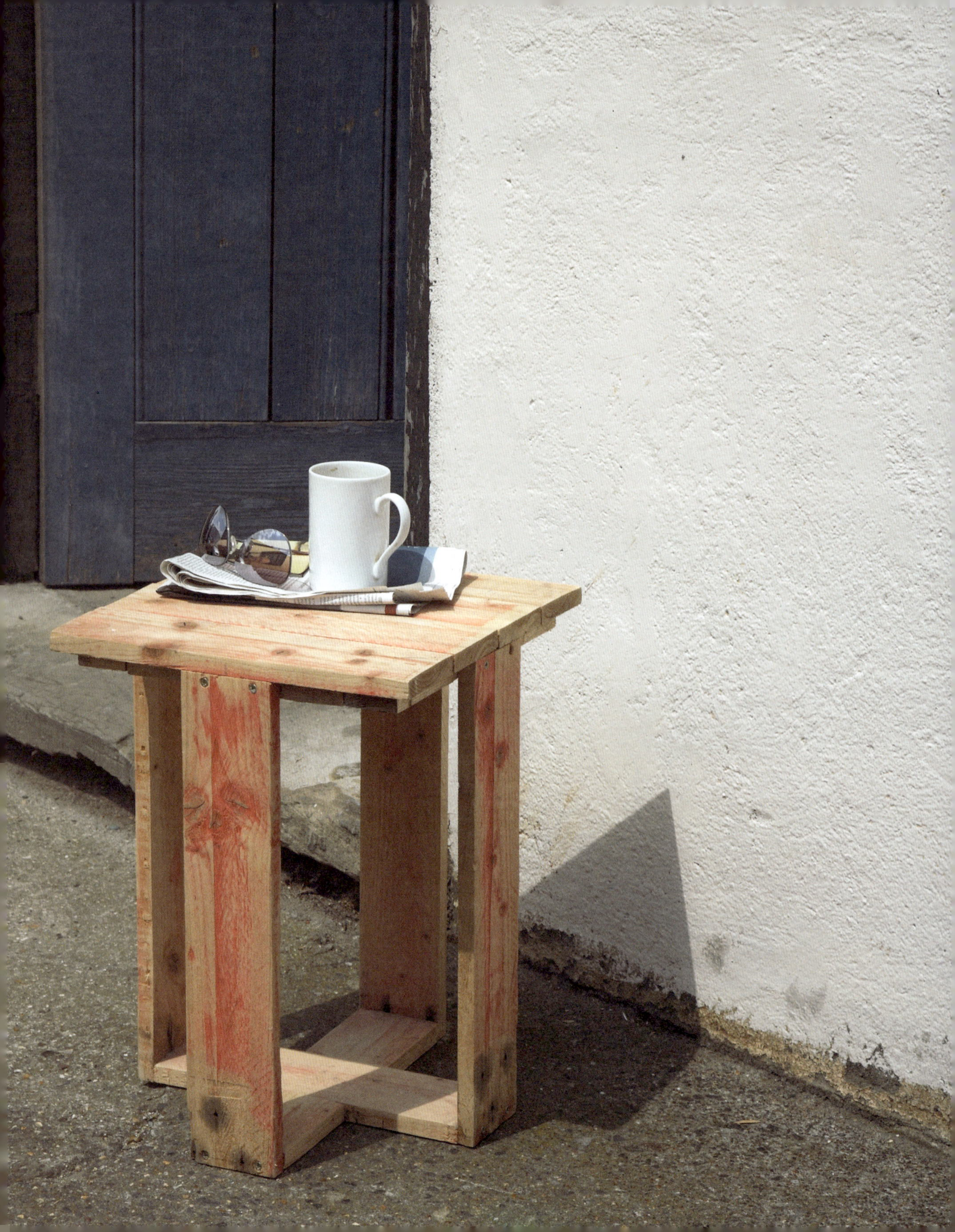

Pallet Stool

I'm interested in ways of reusing discarded materials and objects. I made this stool out of wood from abandoned pallets – a good source of free wood – but it can be made with any kind of wood that fits the dimensions. The stool could also be used as a side table. Shops receive deliveries of goods on pallets: sometimes these are reused, but often they are thrown away. Ask your local shopkeepers whether they have any pallets that you may take.

Instructions

WHAT YOU NEED

Wood
    16 x 87mm (5/8 x 3 1/2in) section: 4m 25cm (14ft)
    16 x 62mm (5/8 x 2 1/2in) section: 1m 55cm (5ft 1in)
Screws: 36 with countersunk heads,
    3.5mm gauge x 30mm long (size 6, 1 1/4in)
Wood glue
Sandpaper

Saw
Drill
Clearance-countersink bit: 3mm
Chisel
Screwdriver
Try square

TECHNIQUES

Measuring and marking: see page 86
Sawing wood: see pages 86–7, 92
Planing and sanding: see pages 87, 92
Drilling holes: see pages 88–9, 92
Gluing and clamping: see pages 93 and 90
Cross-halving joints: see page 94

1

Cut out the following elements. The easiest way to do it is with a bench table saw; a jigsaw is also fine, as is an old-fashioned saw – but this will take lot of arm muscle and patience.
Legs: four pieces, 430 x 87mm (1ft 5in x 3 1/2in)
Seat slats: four pieces, 350 x 87mm (1ft 1 3/4in x 3 1/2in)
Stool base: two pieces, 310 x 87mm (12 3/16in x 3 1/2in)
Under-seat slats: five pieces, 310 x 62mm (12 3/16 x 2 1/2in).

For the under-seat slats, you can use any width of wood as long as it makes a finished square of 310 x 310mm (12 3/16 x 12 3/16in).

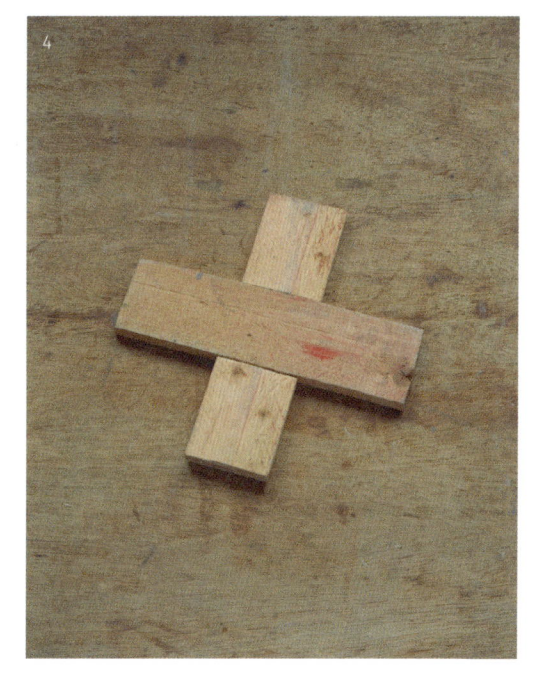

2

Prepare the five under-seat slats. Drill and countersink the holes for attaching the under-seat slats to the seat slats. I made four holes, evenly positioned along each under-seat slat.

3

Prepare the four legs. Drill and countersink the holes for attaching the legs to the under-seat slats and the stool base: make two holes in each end of the leg – 8mm ($5/16$in) in from the short end and 20mm ($3/4$in) in from the side.

4

The two pieces for the base of the stool fit together in a cross shape with a flush surface, so the central portion of each has to be chiselled out to allow them to be joined together. This is known as a cross-halving joint. Use a saw to make at least five cuts halfway through the thickness of the wood, and then chisel out (see page 94). The chiselled area is in the centre of each piece, and starts 111mm ($4^5/16$in) from each end. Put the pieces together (dry – no glue) and test for fit.

PALLET STOOL

Instructions

5

Now you are ready to assemble the stool; use the try square to check that everything is square. Take the four seat slats and glue together along the long edges. Clamp and leave for 20 minutes, while the glue dries. Screw the under-seat slats to the base of the seat.

6

Connect the pieces for the stool base: press the pieces together to form a cross, using glue in the central portion. Clamp and leave to dry for 20 minutes. Screw the top of the legs to the under-seat slats, positioning each leg in the centre of the run of under-seat slats.

7

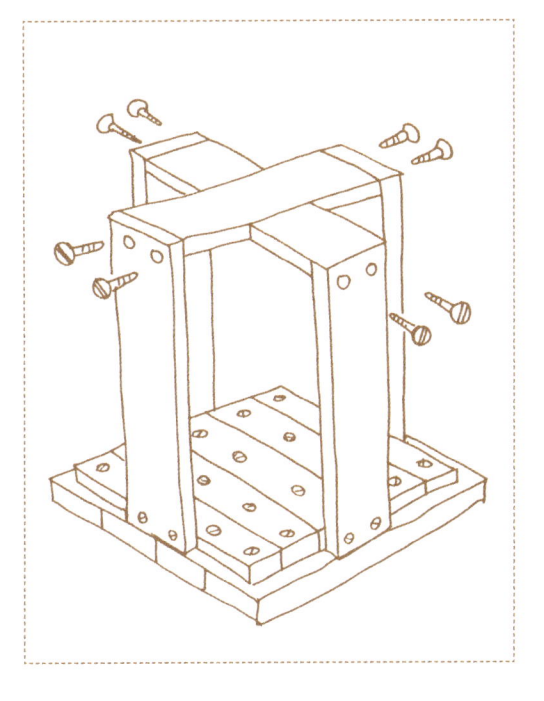

Place the stool base within the four legs, and screw the base of each leg to the end of the crossed pieces. Give the stool a light sanding.

8

The rustic look of this stool is part of its charm. It also makes a very easily portable side table, which is ideal for use in the garden. If you wish to apply a finish, see page 91. Any table that will be used for food must only be treated with a suitable non-toxic finish.

PALLET STOOL 27

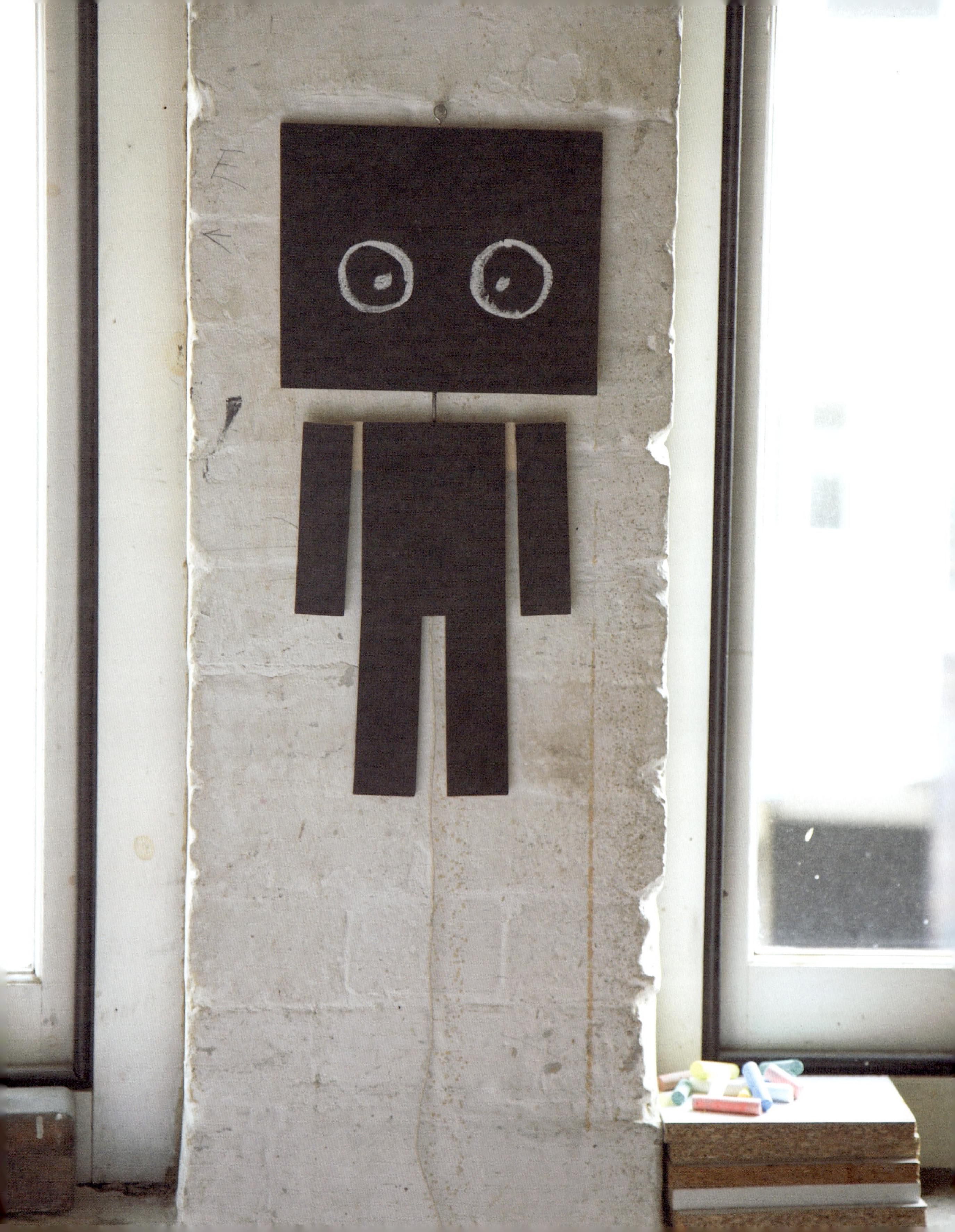

Blackboard Robot

I've got happy childhood memories of playing with jumping jack puppets that my father made for me. Here I have made my own robot version, which is painted with blackboard paint. Children will love chalking on the robot's features, and changing its expression at will; it can also be used as a noticeboard. Using this model, you could make different kinds of figures by adjusting the sizes and shapes of the body parts. It is a good idea to cut out the shapes in cardboard to experiment with, before cutting them in wood.

Instructions

WHAT YOU NEED

Plywood, 6mm (1/4in) thick:
   350 x 250mm (1ft 1 3/4in x 10in)
String
Inside of a net curtain wire – the coiled
   metal part: small piece
Blackboard paint
Eye hooks: two x 5mm eye, one x 10mm eye
Screws: 6 part-threaded, 3mm gauge x
   12mm long (size 4 x 1/2in)
Masking tape
Wood glue
Cocktail stick or match

Saw
Paintbrush
Drill
Flat drill bit: 2mm
Hammer
Screwdriver

TECHNIQUES

Measuring and marking: see page 86
Sawing wood: see pages 86–7, 92
Planing and sanding: see pages 87, 92
Drilling holes: see pages 88–9, 92
Gluing and clamping: see pages 93 and 90
Finishes for wood: see page 91

Template for arm connectors.

30 One Piece of Wood

1

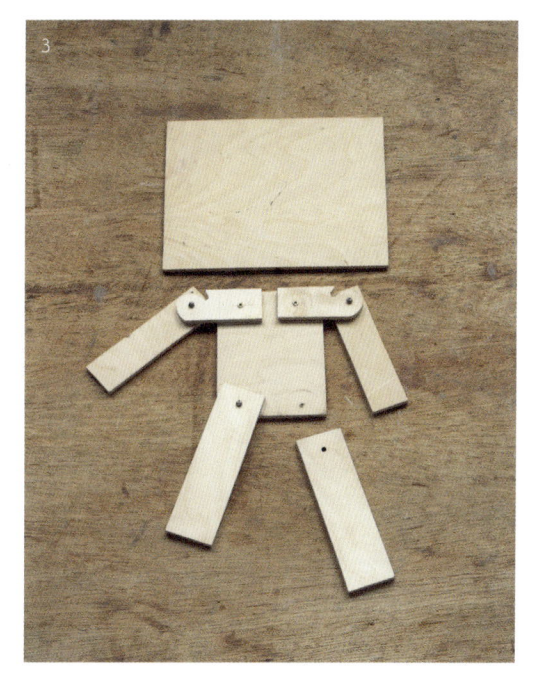

Draw the following pieces on the plywood and cut out with the saw.
Head: 180 x 225mm (7 x 9in)
Body: 100 x 135mm (4 x 5$^{1}/_{4}$in)
Arms: two pieces, 35 x 135mm (1$^{1}/_{4}$ x 5$^{1}/_{2}$in)
Legs: two pieces, 45 x 150mm (1$^{3}/_{4}$ x 6in)
Arm connectors: two, cut out as per template

2

Paint the front of the head, body, arms and legs with blackboard paint – put masking tape around the edges to prevent paint getting on these areas.

3

Now you are ready to put the robot man together. Put a bit of glue on the back of the arm connectors, and position them on the back of the body in the shoulder area, with the curved side uppermost and facing outwards, flush with the top of the body and protruding 40mm (1$^{1}/_{2}$in) from it. Screw the arm connectors tightly to the back of body.

Drill a hole, 10mm ($^{3}/_{8}$in) deep, in the top edge of each leg (to house the string that connects the legs). Position it 8mm ($^{3}/_{8}$in) from the outer edge. Place a leg on each side at the base of the back of the body: the top should be 25mm (1in) away from the base of the body. Screw on the legs, making sure they remain loose enough to move freely. It is important to use part-threaded screws, as the unthreaded part allows the legs to swing easily.

BLACKBOARD ROBOT

4

Join the head to the body, on their edges, with a piece of net curtain wire. Mark the centre top of the body and the centre of the base of the head. Drill a hole about 15mm (5/8in) deep. Take care to drill straight. Fill the drill holes with glue and push in a piece of curtain wire.

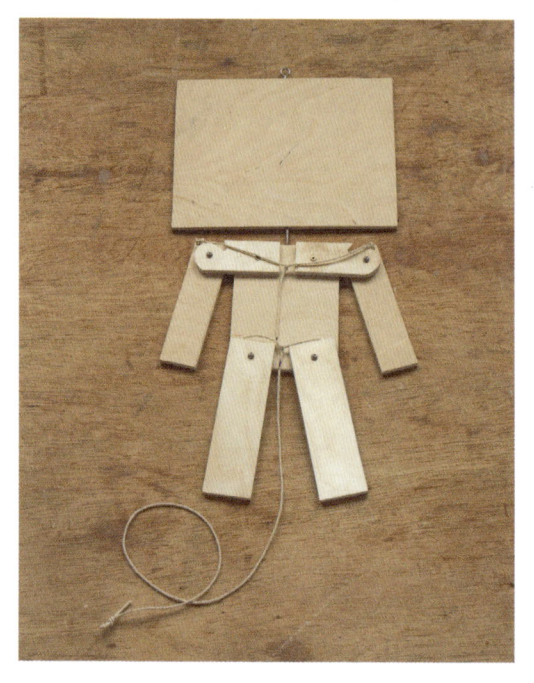

5

It is now time to add the string that allows you to move the robot's arms and legs. Screw a small eye in the top outer corner of the back of each arm. Fasten a piece of string between the two, but don't make it too tight.

Cut a piece of string to loosely connect the tops of the legs. Squirt some glue down each hole, then push one end of the string inside and carefully bang in a piece of cocktail stick or matchstick to hold the string in place.

Attach the 'pull' string that connects and operates the arm and leg strings. Tie it in the centre of the arm strings, run it down to knot in the centre of the leg strings, and leave a tail of about 500mm (20in). Screw the big eye in the centre of the top of the head to hang the robot.

TIP

YOU CAN MAKE DIFFERENT FIGURES. CUT THEM OUT IN PAPER OR CARDBOARD FIRST SO YOU CAN PLAY AROUND WITH VARIOUS DESIGNS.

Blackboard Robot

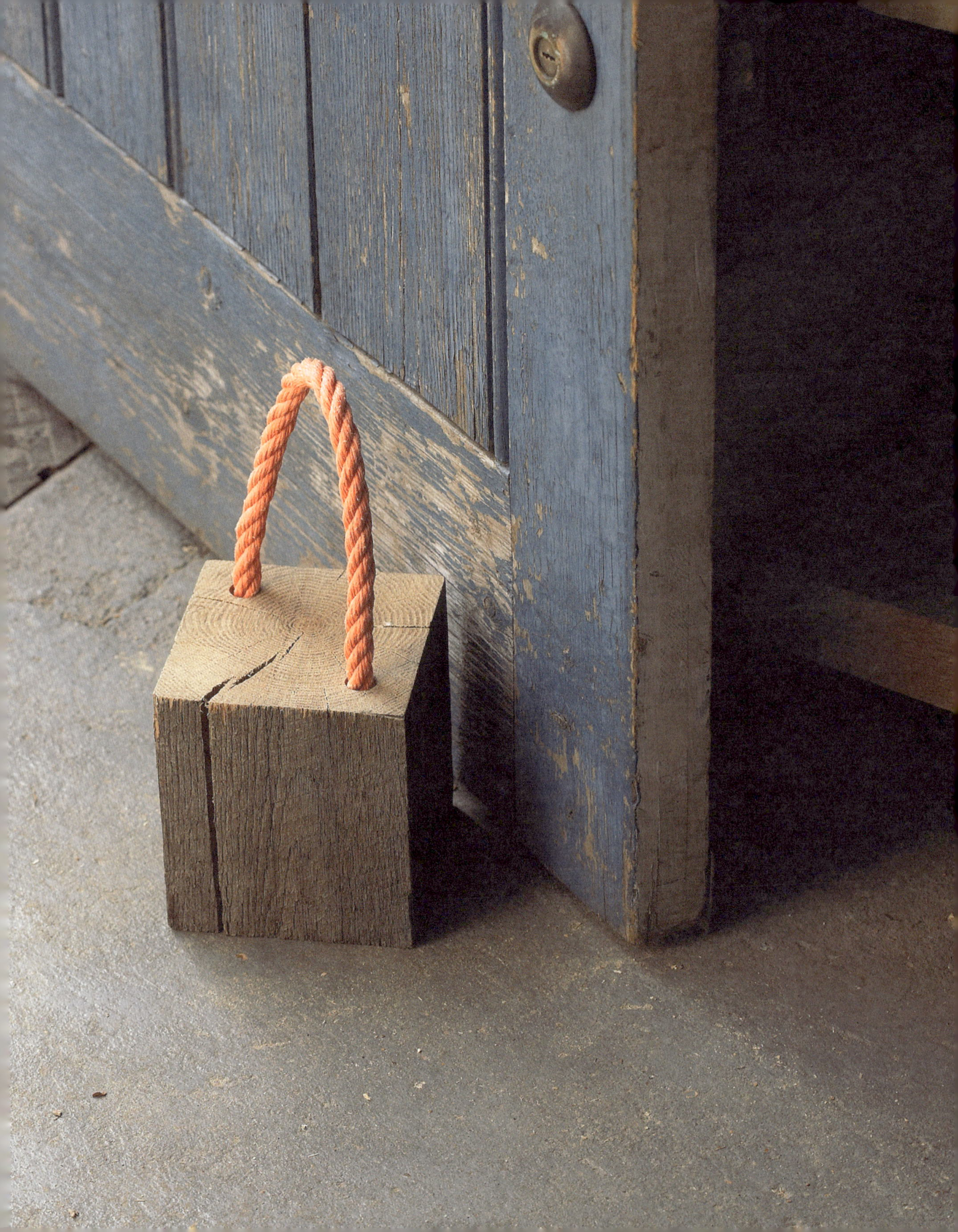

Doorstop Block

I use doorstops everywhere. I find the contrast of the rawness of timber with a clean cut very appealing. Thick rope is used to make a handy handle, and I often use the doorstops for other things such as holding down paper from a roll. You can make a doorstop out of any big, heavy block of wood. A piece of hardwood is best, as it will be heavier than softwood. Here, I have used wood from an old oak beam that came out of a house that was being demolished.

Instructions

WHAT YOU NEED

Block of wood: around 130 x 130 x 130mm (5 x 5 x 5in)
Thick rope, about 12mm ($^1/_2$in) in diameter: 1m (1yd)
Duct tape (or similar; for binding end of rope)

Saw
Plane
Drill
Flat drill bit: 13mm
Hinge-cutter or Forstner drill bit: 35mm

TECHNIQUES

Measuring and marking: see page 86
Sawing wood: see pages 86-7, 92
Planing and sanding: see pages 87, 92
Drilling holes: see pages 88-9, 92

CUT BLOCK THIS SIZE

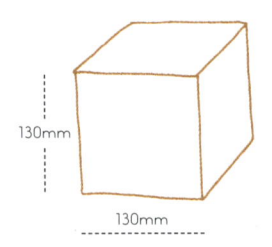

130mm
130mm

DRILL HOLES IN TOP OF BLOCK

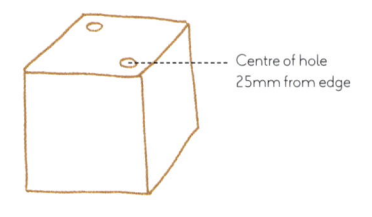

Centre of hole 25mm from edge

DRILL BIGGER HOLES IN BASE OF BLOCK

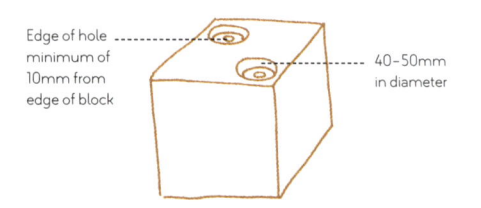

Edge of hole minimum of 10mm from edge of block

40-50mm in diameter

1

The main issue in making this doorstop is getting the wood cut into a square. With a bit of hard work, it can be done with a hand-saw. It is not easy to get it straight, but you can use a plane after it has been cut if you need to square it up. Most domestic electrical saws do not have blades that are big enough to cut a piece like this, but you could get a local timber merchant or carpenter to cut it to size.

2

Drill a hole right through the block in two diagonally opposite corners, centring the hole 25mm (1in) from the edge. (The hole needs to be a couple of millimetres bigger than the diameter of the rope.)

One Piece of Wood

3

On the underside of the block, use the hinge-cutter or Forstner bit to drill a bigger hole – around 40–50mm (1³⁄₄–2in) in diameter and 15–20mm (⁵⁄₈–³⁄₄in) deep – that will contain the knotted end of the rope. Centre these holes on the original drilled holes. The edge of the hole should be a minimum of 10mm (³⁄₈in) from the edge of the block, to make sure the edge remains strong enough.

4

You are now ready to thread the rope through the block to make a handle. Knot each end of the rope so the handle is the length you want.

5

Rope is available in colours, as well as the natural colour. Bind the end with tape to stop it fraying.

DOORSTOP BLOCK

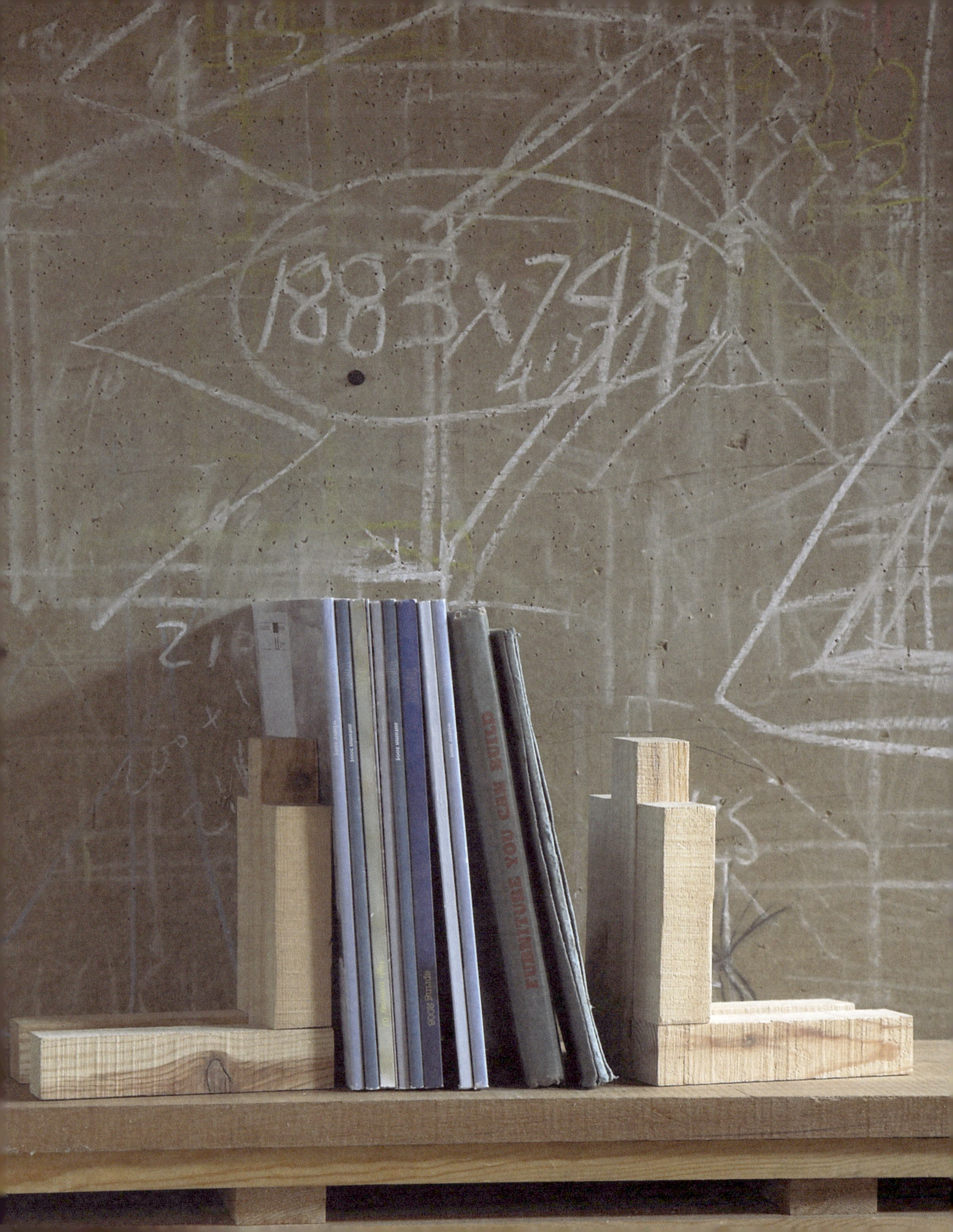
FURNITURE YOU CAN BUILD

Robot Bookends

These bookends began life as a practical solution to stop books falling on people's heads, but they can add an element of fun to any home or office. The robot idea came about as I was playing with some sticks of wood and suddenly a robot was sitting on the table. Two of these quirky little characters sitting back to back are perfect for holding small books or a stack of letters. I have used pine, but you can use any kind of wood you like.

Instructions

WHAT YOU NEED

Wood: 30 x 30mm (1¼ x 1¼in) section – about 690mm (2ft 3in) long (per bookend)
Wood glue
Sandpaper (optional)

Saw
Nail or sharp object to make the eyes with
Clamps

TECHNIQUES

Measuring and marking: see page 86
Sawing wood: see pages 86–7, 92
Planing and sanding: see pages 87, 92
Drilling holes: see pages 88–9, 92
Gluing and clamping: see pages 93 and 90

1

For each bookend, cut the wood to the following lengths.
Head/body: one piece, 170mm (7in) long
Legs: two pieces, 150mm (6in) long
Arms: two pieces, 110mm (4¼in) long

2

If you want a very smooth finish, sand all the pieces. Use the nail to inscribe a small circle with a hole at the centre, to form the robot's eyes at the top end of the head/body piece.

One Piece of Wood

3

Now glue the pieces together. Make sure all surfaces are straight and free from dirt. Spread the wood glue evenly on the sides to be joined with a brush, stick or glue spreader. The head/ body stands upright, with the legs on either side, sticking out at 90°. The arms are positioned vertically next to the body, and sit on top of the legs.

4

Clamp the joints together, but not so tightly that all the glue is squeezed out. Check that the robot is held correctly, with the surfaces straight and the joints flush. Clean off excess glue – I normally use a wetted old toothbrush, but a tissue will do. It should be dry within 20–30 minutes, depending on the type of glue.

PATINATION OF METALS
HANDBOOK
Moderne Vergangenheit
MAGIC

Elegant Trestle

I really like trestles and I have made quite a lot of them. I always keep an eye out for home-made trestles in other people's workshops and on building sites. This trestle has been inspired by my observations of these simple, functional structures. The quantities given are for one trestle, and you will need at least two to support a tabletop. The minimum size of tabletop that two trestles will hold is 80cm x 1m (2ft 8in x 3ft 3in); the maximum is 120cm x 2m 30cm (4ft x 7ft 6in). Trestles give you great flexibility: add more trestles for a bigger tabletop, or use them to create an L-shaped table, for example. I cut this wood section out of a discarded pine scaffolding plank that I found.

Instructions

WHAT YOU NEED

Wood – pine: 4m 80cm x 30mm x 30mm
  (15ft 9in x 1¼in x 1¼in) (per trestle)
Wooden dowels: 12, 30mm
  (1¼in) long x 6mm (¼in) in diameter
Wood glue

Saw
Drill
Flat drill bit: 6mm
Pilot-countersink bit: 6mm
Dowelling jig kit (optional)

Mallet
Try square

TECHNIQUES

Measuring and marking: see page 86
Sawing wood: see pages 86–7, 92
Planing and sanding: see pages 87, 92
Drilling holes: see pages 88–9, 92
Gluing and clamping: see pages 93 and 90
Finishes for wood: see page 91
Dowelled joints: see pages 93, 94

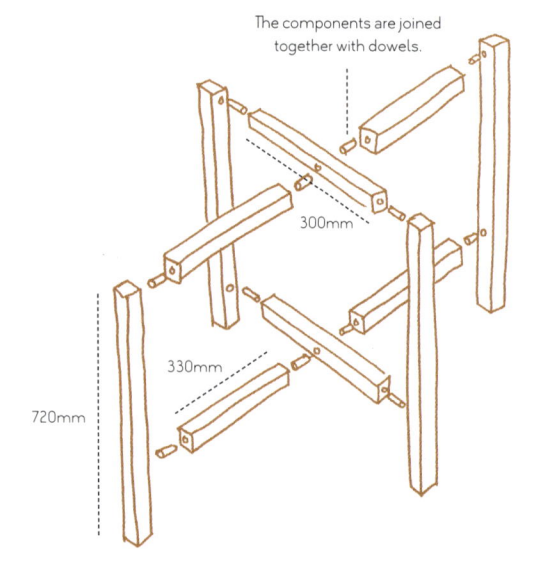

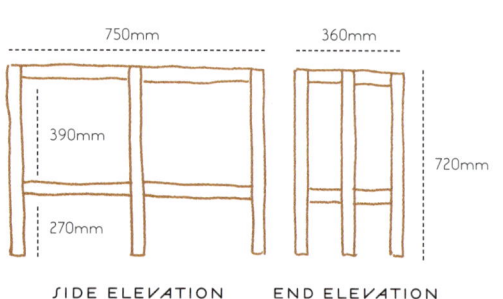

The components are joined together with dowels.

300mm
330mm
720mm

750mm
390mm
270mm
SIDE ELEVATION

360mm
720mm
END ELEVATION

1

Cut the wood into the following lengths.
Legs: four pieces, 720mm (2ft 4½in) long
Long crossbar: four pieces, 330mm (13in) long
Short crossbar: two pieces, 300mm (12in) long

2

Make the holes for the dowels that join the pieces together, centring them on the ends of the crossbars and making corresponding holes in the legs. There is one dowel for each joint. If you do not have a dowel jig kit, make a jig (see page 93) out of some scrap wood.

Drill the holes in the positions shown, using the flat drill bit – drill through the jig 15mm (⅝in) into the wood. Take the wood out of the jig and use the countersink bit to countersink the holes.

44 One Piece of Wood

3

Join the pieces together with the dowels – make the two crossbars first and then add the four legs. Squirt glue into the holes and tap in the dowel with the mallet, and then push it into the hole in the corresponding piece.

4

Use a try square to check that all the corners are square, and then leave glued parts to dry for a minimum of 20 minutes.

ELEGANT TRESTLE

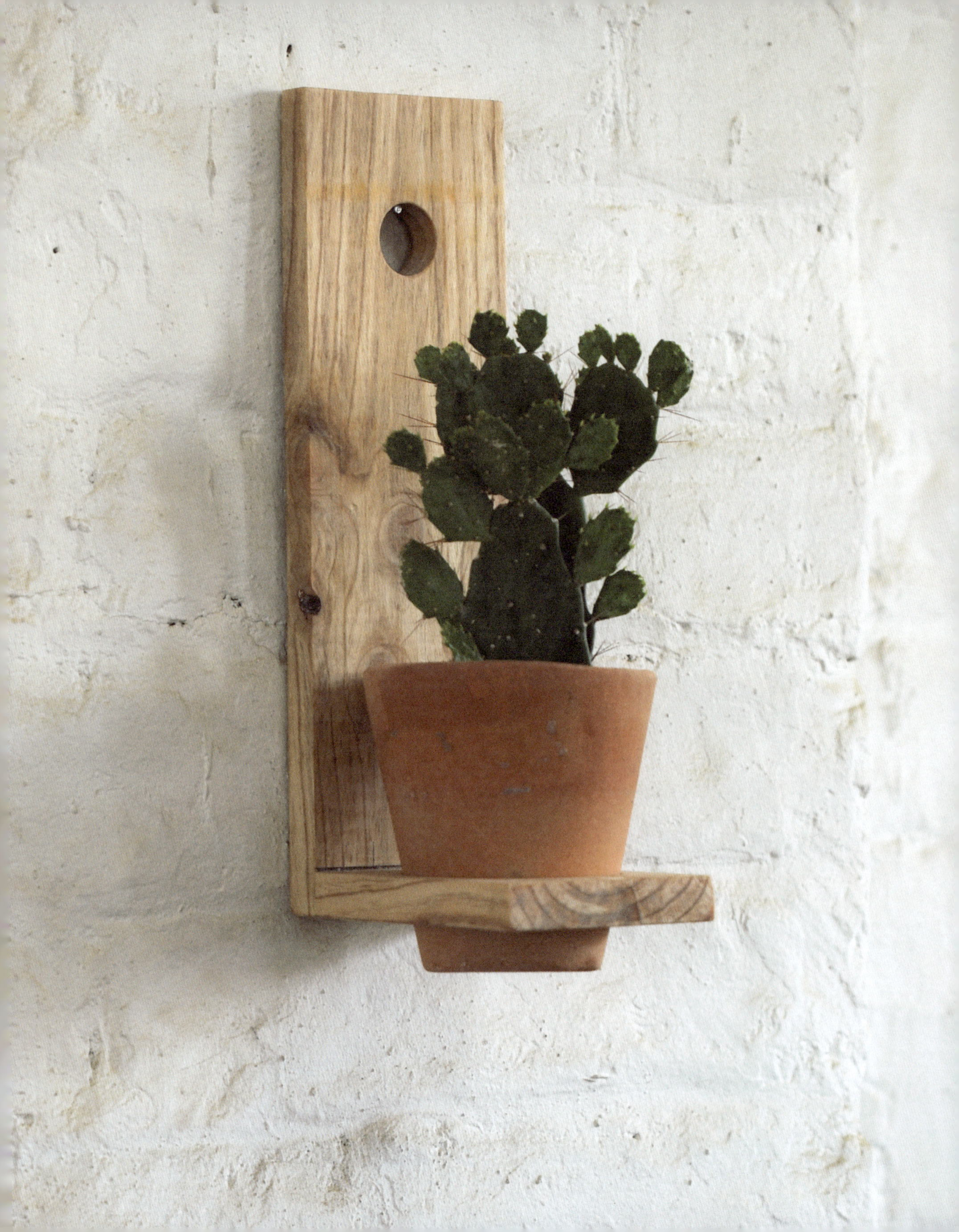

Plant Holder

This wall planter can be hung indoors or outdoors. I quite like to hang several of them together as a vertical garden, which looks great. The planter shape can be used for different purposes, too – add a nice cup and use it to store toothbrushes in the bathroom or utensils in the kitchen. For the wood, use pine or any scrap wood or offcuts. I have cut the pieces from an old pine plank.

Instructions

WHAT YOU NEED

Wood: 400 x 90 x 15mm (1ft 4in x 3$\frac{1}{2}$in x $\frac{5}{8}$in)
Screws: 3 screws with countersunk head, 4mm gauge x 30mm long (size 8 x 1$\frac{1}{4}$in)
Wood glue
Small terracotta plant pot, 100mm (4in) in diameter at the widest part

Saw
Drill
Flat wood drill bit: 25mm
Pilot-countersink bit: 3mm
Holesaw: 70mm

TECHNIQUES

Measuring and marking: see page 86
Sawing wood: see pages 86-7, 92
Planing and sanding: see pages 87, 92
Drilling holes: see pages 88-9, 92
Gluing and clamping: see pages 93 and 90
Finishes for wood: see page 91
Finger joints: see page 95

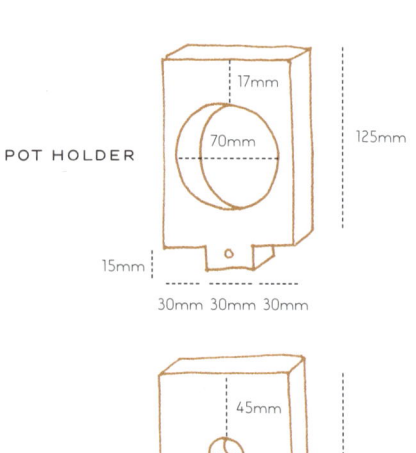

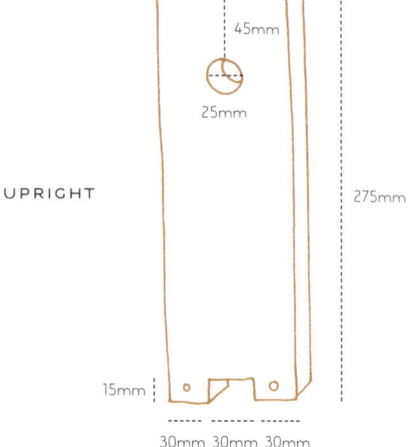

POT HOLDER
17mm
70mm
125mm
15mm
30mm 30mm 30mm

UPRIGHT
45mm
25mm
275mm
15mm
30mm 30mm 30mm

48 One Piece of Wood

1

Cut the wood into two pieces, 275 mm (11in) long (for the upright) and 125 mm (5in) long (for the pot holder).

2

Using the 25mm drill bit, drill a hanging hole at the top of the upright, 45mm (1½in) from the top edge and centred. Use the holesaw to cut the hole in the pot holder, positioning it 17mm (¾in) from what will be the front edge of the plant holder, and centring it.

3

Cut out the finger joints (see page 95) in the pot holder and upright. The pot holder has a tongue 30mm (1¼in) wide, which protrudes 15mm (⅝in). The upright has a matching cutaway portion, 30mm (1¼in) wide and 15mm (⅝in) deep.

On the back of the base of the upright, drill and countersink two small holes with the 3mm drill bit. Position the holes 7mm (⅜in) from the bottom edge and 20mm (¾in) from the side edges, and drill right through the upright. With the pot holder lying wrong side uppermost, drill a similar hole in the tongue, positioning it 20mm (¾in) from the edge of the tongue and equidistant from the side edges.

4

Spread a bit of glue on the end of the joining pieces, and push the pot holder into the upright. Screw the pieces together through the back of the upright and the underside of the pot holder.

PLANT HOLDER

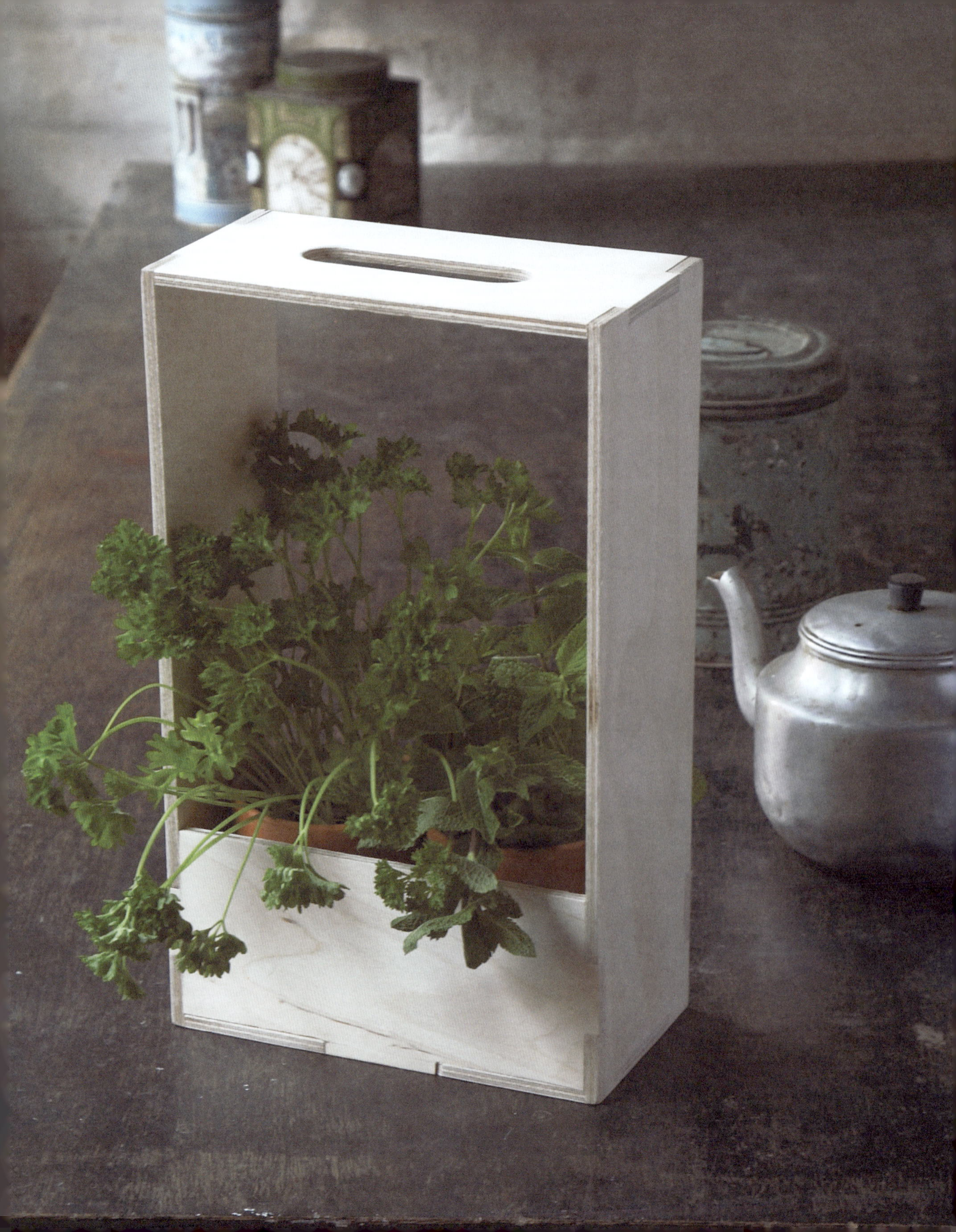

Herb Carrier

I love to have pots of herbs in the kitchen, both for cooking and for using fresh in salads. When you buy herb plants in the supermarket, they come in unattractive black plastic containers, so I designed this herb carrier to keep my herbs in. It looks good enough to put on the dinner table, but also allows me to take it to where I'm cooking, put it outside on a sunny day, or just move it around on the window ledge.

Instructions

What You Need

Birch plywood, 6mm (¼in thick):
　　550 x 350mm (1ft 9½ x 1ft 1¾in)
Wood glue
Terracotta pot and saucer:
　　two, max. 9cm (3½in) in diameter
Parcel tape
Sandpaper or half-round wood file

Small toolbox saw or 165mm (6½in) pullsaw
Drill
Flat wood bit: 25mm

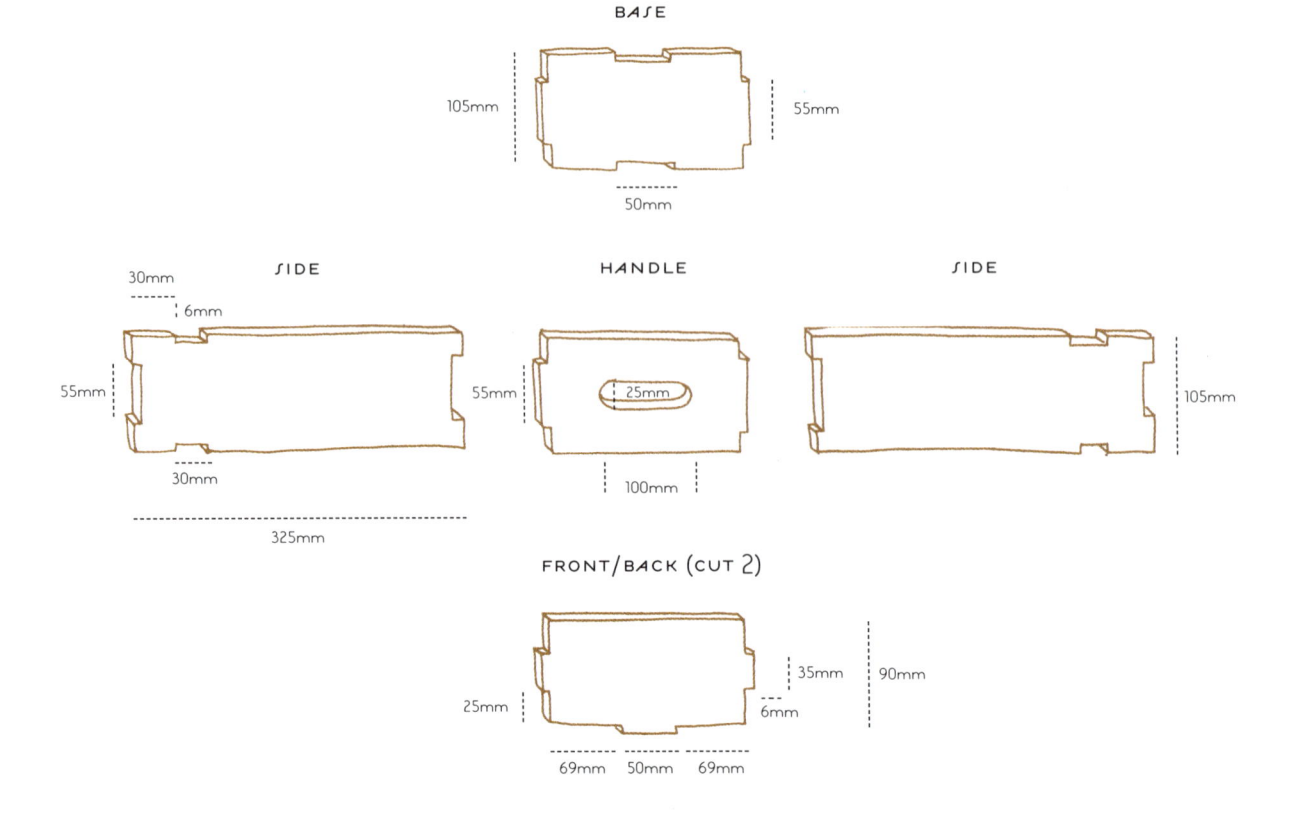

Techniques

Measuring and marking: see page 86
Sawing wood: see pages 86-7, 92
Planing and sanding: see pages 87, 92
Drilling holes: see pages 88-9, 92
Gluing and clamping: see pages 93 and 90
Finger joints: see page 95

BASE
105mm · 55mm · 50mm

SIDE
30mm · 6mm · 55mm · 30mm · 325mm

HANDLE
55mm · 25mm · 100mm

SIDE
105mm

FRONT/BACK (CUT 2)
25mm · 35mm · 6mm · 90mm · 69mm · 50mm · 69mm

The length of each piece for the front/back, handle and base is 200mm including the tongues. Each tongue protrudes 6mm.

52　One Piece of Wood

1

Referring to the diagram, draw the two side pieces, front and back pieces, handle and base on the plywood and cut them out.

2

Draw the handle hole in the handle piece. Position it 50mm (2in) from each short end, and 40mm (1½in) from each long side; the handle hole is 25mm (1in) wide. Drill a 25mm (1in) hole at each end, centring the drill 62mm (2⁷/16in) from each short end and 50mm (2in) in from the long side.

Instructions

3

Cut out the handle shape with the saw. Give the edges of the handle hole a light sanding (or use a file to smooth the edges).

4

Cut out the finger joints in each of the six components, according to the measurements on the diagram.

5

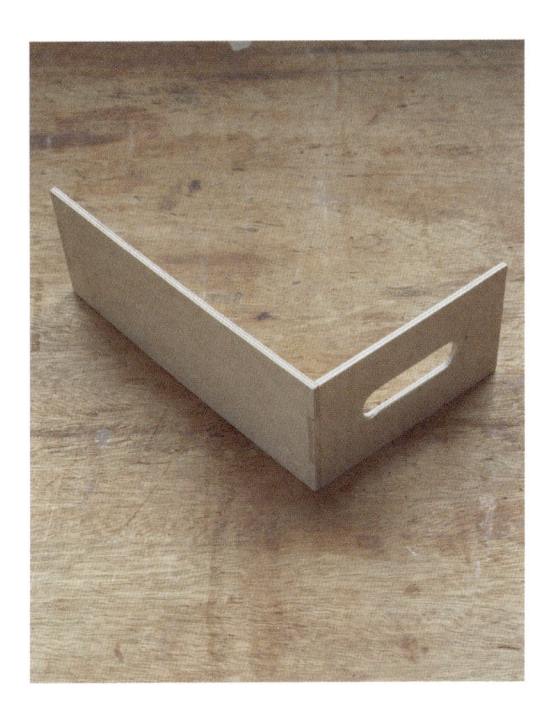

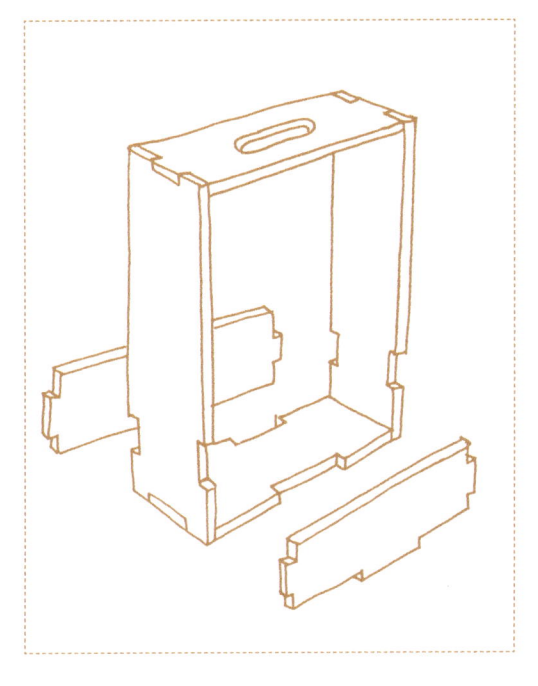

Pencil-mark the ends of the pieces that are to be glued together, as it is easy to make a mistake. Glue the pieces and click them together: make the frame part of the herb carrier first by slotting together the long sides, handle and base. Encircle the frame with parcel tape to hold everything together until the glue dries.

6

Add the front and back piece; keep these in place with parcel tape also, until dry. Place the plant pots of herbs and their saucers in the herb carrier and put in a light position.

Herb Carrier

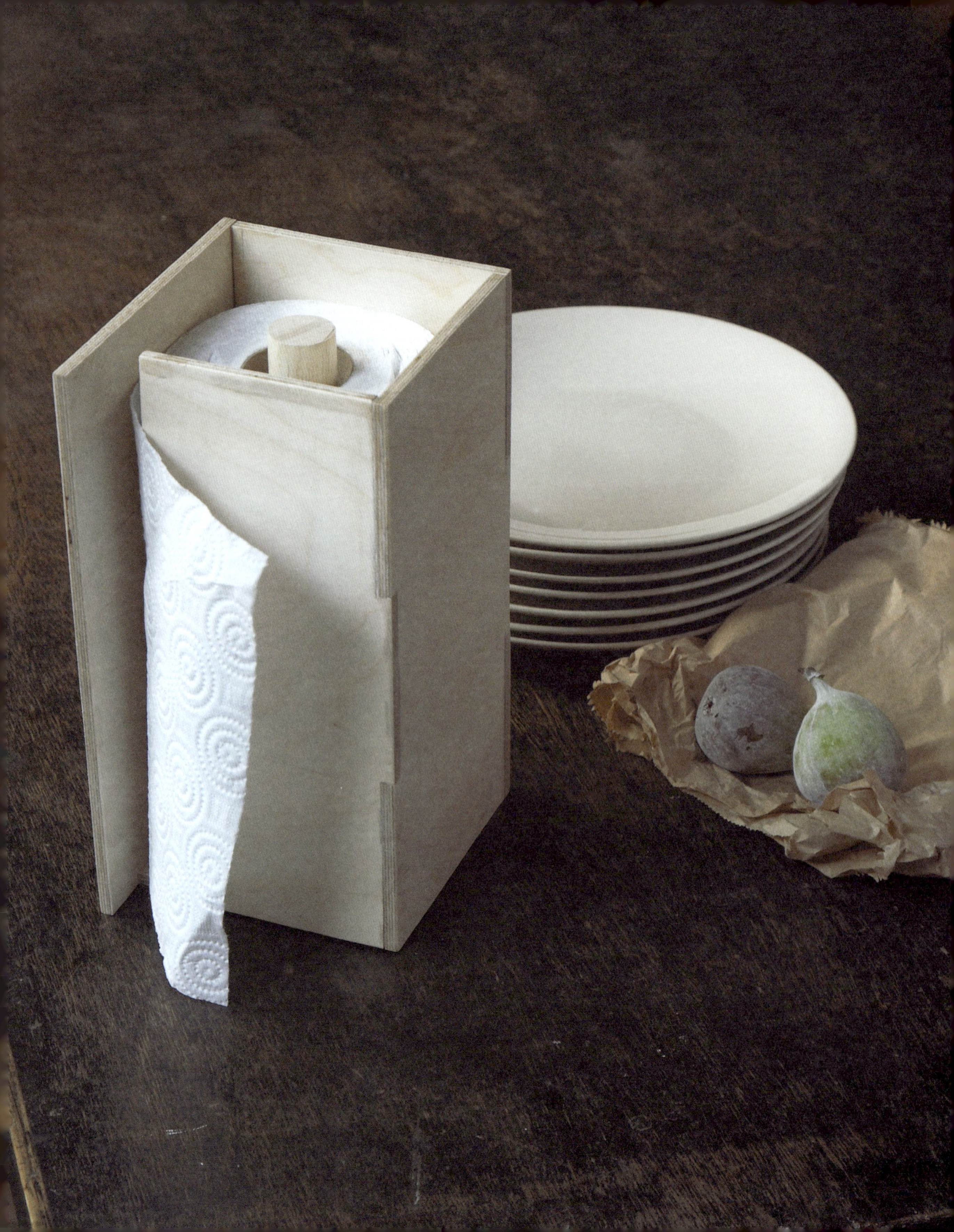

Kitchen Roll Holder

Kitchen roll holders are generally fairly unimaginative and not very appealing, but this attractive design will blend stylishly into any kitchen. It conceals a kitchen roll inside, but allows you to pull out and tear off a sheet of paper as you need it. Its other great advantage is that it is portable, so you can move it when you need it close at hand.

Instructions

WHAT YOU NEED

Birch plywood: 6mm (¼in) thick, 675 x 245mm (1ft 2½in x 9½in) or 500 x 380mm (1ft 7¾in x 1ft 3in)
Broomstick dowelling: 230mm (9in) long and about 25mm (1in) in diameter
Screw: 1 with countersunk head, 3mm gauge x 30mm long (size 4, 1¼in)
Wood glue
Sandpaper

Small toolbox saw or bandsaw
Drill
Pilot-countersink bit: 3mm
Screwdriver
Clamps
Try square

TECHNIQUES

Measuring and marking: see page 86
Sawing wood: see pages 86–7, 92
Planing and sanding: see pages 87, 92
Drilling holes: see pages 88–9, 92
Gluing and clamping: see pages 93 and 90
Finger joints: see page 95

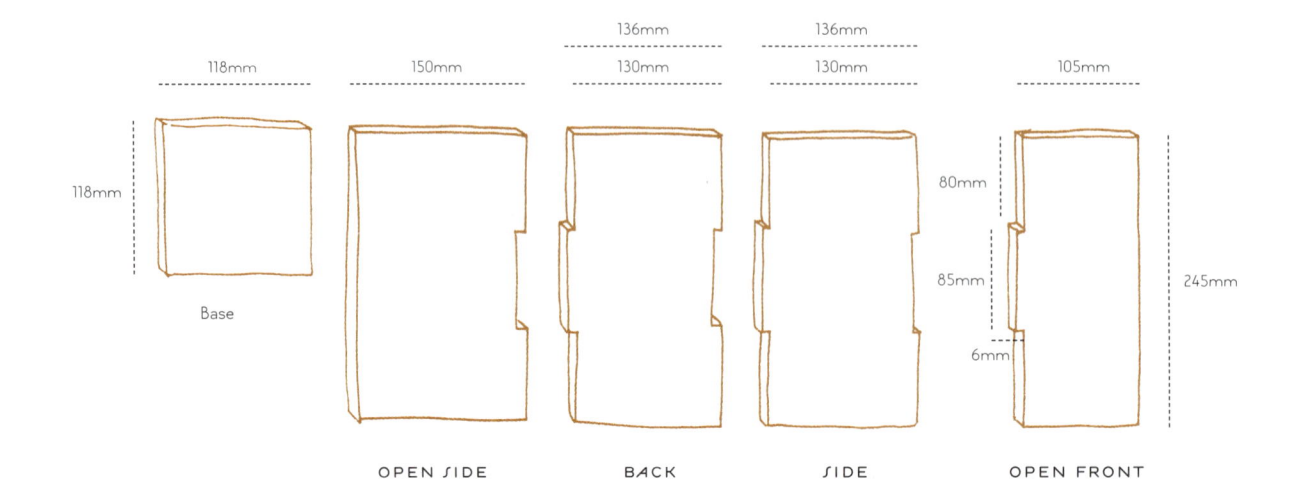

Base — 118mm x 118mm
Open side — 150mm wide
Back — 136mm / 130mm
Side — 136mm / 130mm
Open front — 105mm wide; 80mm, 85mm, 6mm; 245mm tall

Dowelling for kitchen roll — 230mm x 25mm

1

Referring to the diagram, draw the base, open front, back, side and open side pieces on the plywood and cut them out.

58 One Piece of Wood

2

On the reverse of the base, rule a line between each corner to find the centre of the piece. Drill a hole through it with the pilot-countersink bit.

Drill and countersink a pilot hole in one end of the dowelling, to a depth of 30mm (1½in). Attach the dowelling to the base by screwing through from the underside of the base until the dowel is joined tightly to the base.

3

Pencil-mark the parts of the pieces that are to be glued together, as it is easy to make a mistake. Glue the walls and base together, slotting the pieces into each other as illustrated.

4

Use clamps to gently hold the kitchen roll holder together, check that the corners are square, and leave until the glue is dry. Sand lightly to remove excess glue.

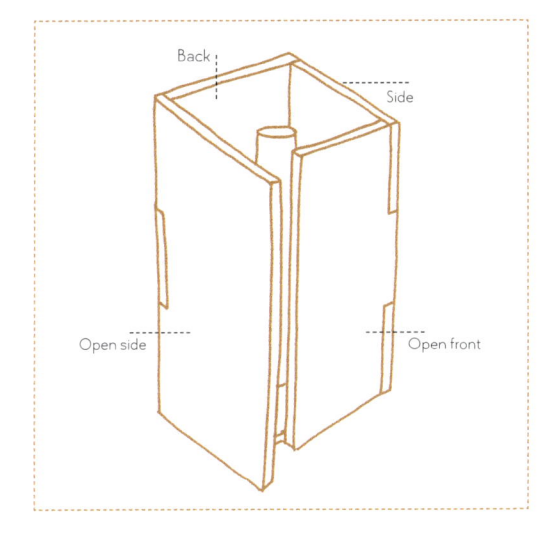

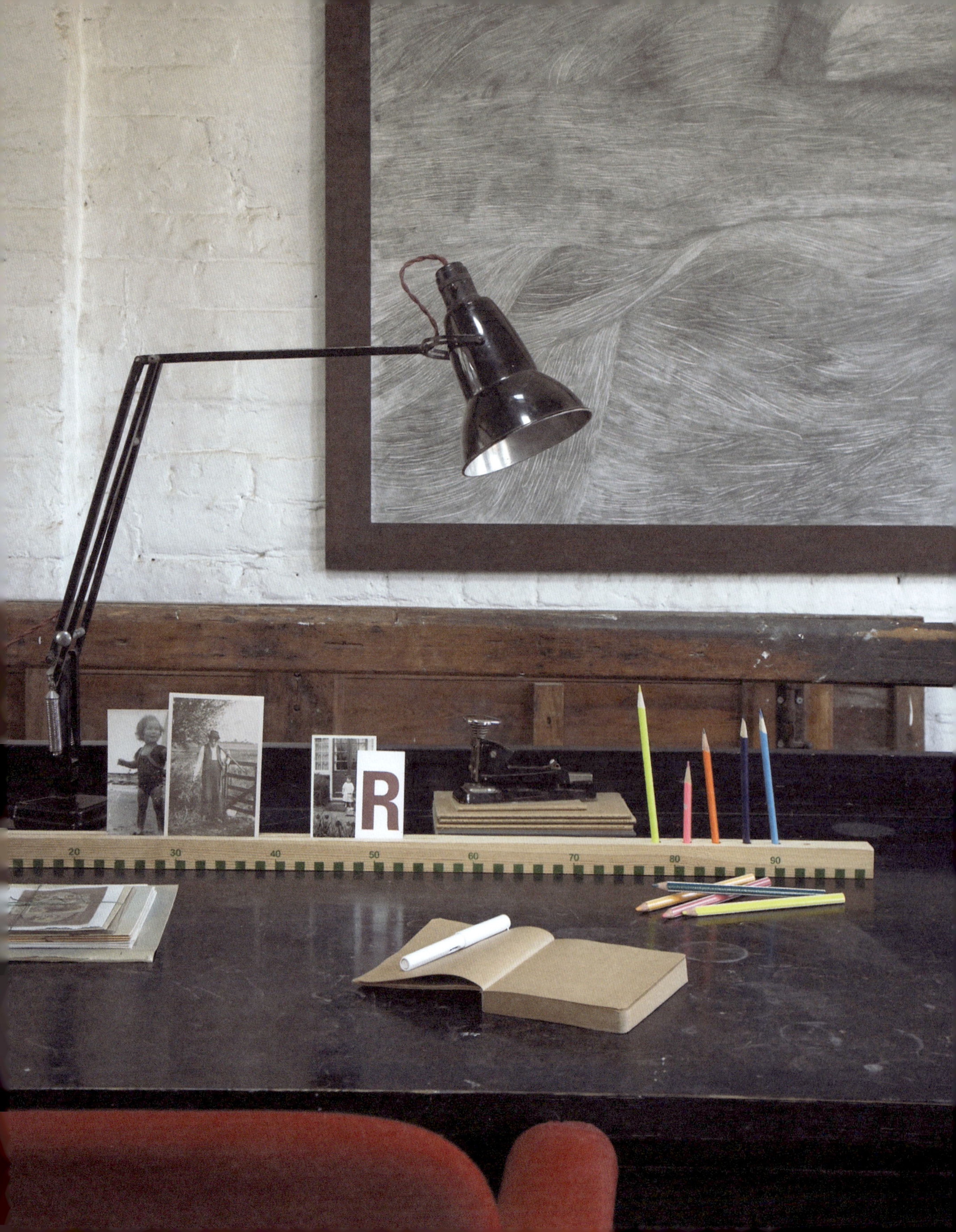
R
20
30
40
50
60
70
80
90

Ruler Display

This ruler blends function and aesthetic appeal. I made it as a way of displaying invitations and postcards and because I like to have some sharp pencils within reach. Every now and then, I also use the ruler to measure fabric that I'm working with. The wood section I've used to make it is a standard size that should be available at your local timber merchant. Its size is described as that of the wood before it is planed; however, it is planed before you buy it, so the actual size is 17 x 32mm ($^5/_8$ x 1$^1/_4$in).

Instructions

What You Need

Wood – 19 x 38mm (³/₄ x 1¹/₂in) section: 2m (6ft)
Wood glue
Masking tape
Leftover paint suitable for wood

Saw
Plane
Chisel
Drill
Drill bit: 8mm
Stanley knife
Small paintbrush
Number stencil (optional)

Techniques

Measuring and marking: see page 86
Sawing wood: see pages 86–7, 92
Planing and sanding: see pages 87, 92
Drilling holes: see pages 88–9, 92
Gluing and clamping: see pages 93 and 90
Finishes for wood: see page 91

Top face of ruler display, showing slot and holes for pencils

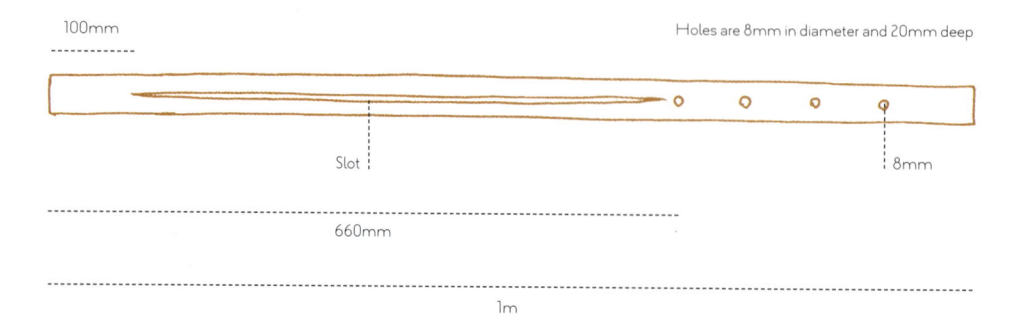

100mm

Holes are 8mm in diameter and 20mm deep

Slot

8mm

660mm

1m

1

Cut the wood into two even pieces, each 1m long (if you're working in imperial, make it as a yardstick).

2

Prepare the slot that will hold cards when the pieces are joined together later. Lay the two pieces with the narrow side uppermost. On one edge, make a mark 100mm (4in) and 660mm (2ft 2in) in from the end. Take the pencil mark over on to the wider face and make a mark 20mm (3/4in) down. (When the two pieces are placed next to each other, the two marked sides should be facing.)

3

You are now going to plane 1mm (1/32in) off each piece where it has been marked. Make a dent with a chisel or knife at the 100mm (4in), 660mm (2ft 2in) and 20mm (3/4in) marks. Fasten each piece to the worktable with clamps. Using a hand plane and starting at the chiselled mark, plane in one direction and then in the other, keeping inside the two chiselled marks. It does not take much planing to remove about 1mm (1/32in).

4

Glue the two pieces together with the planed edges in the centre, forming the slot. Use clamps to hold the pieces together until the glue has dried.

RULER DISPLAY

Instructions

5

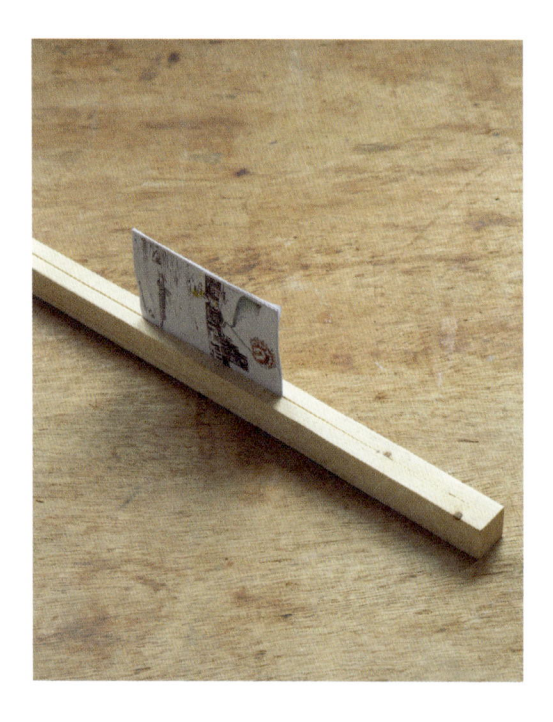

The slot feature will allow you to pop in photos, postcards and other printed matter. Use it for a constantly changing mini gallery of family, friends, upcoming events and day-to-day life.

6

Drill the holes for the pencils. Mark five holes – centred and evenly spaced – at the solid end of the ruler. Mark the drill bit 20mm (3/4in) from the end with a bit of masking tape to make a depth stop that will show you when you have drilled a hole 20mm (3/4in) deep. Use a nail to make an indentation where the hole needs to be drilled – this helps to prevent the drill from moving out of position. As you will be drilling down along the glued joint, it is best to keep the two pieces clamped together as you work.

7

Paint the 1cm gradations along the base of the front face of the ruler (adjust instructions if you are making a yardstick). Run a piece of masking tape along the length of the ruler, 10mm from the lower edge. Find a masking tape that is 10mm wide (or cut pieces to that width) and tape pieces along the lower edge of the ruler with 10mm between each one.

When this is done, make a light cut with a Stanley knife along the edges of the tape that surrounds each area to be painted: this will help prevent the paint from bleeding. Carefully paint the exposed squares of wood. When the paint is dry, take the masking tape off. Use a stencil to paint on numbers if you wish.

TIP

FOR STENCILLING NUMBERS, LOOK FOR A CHILDREN'S LETTER AND NUMBER STENCIL. EXPERIMENT FIRST ON SOME SCRAP WOOD BEFORE ATTEMPTING TO PAINT THE RULER.

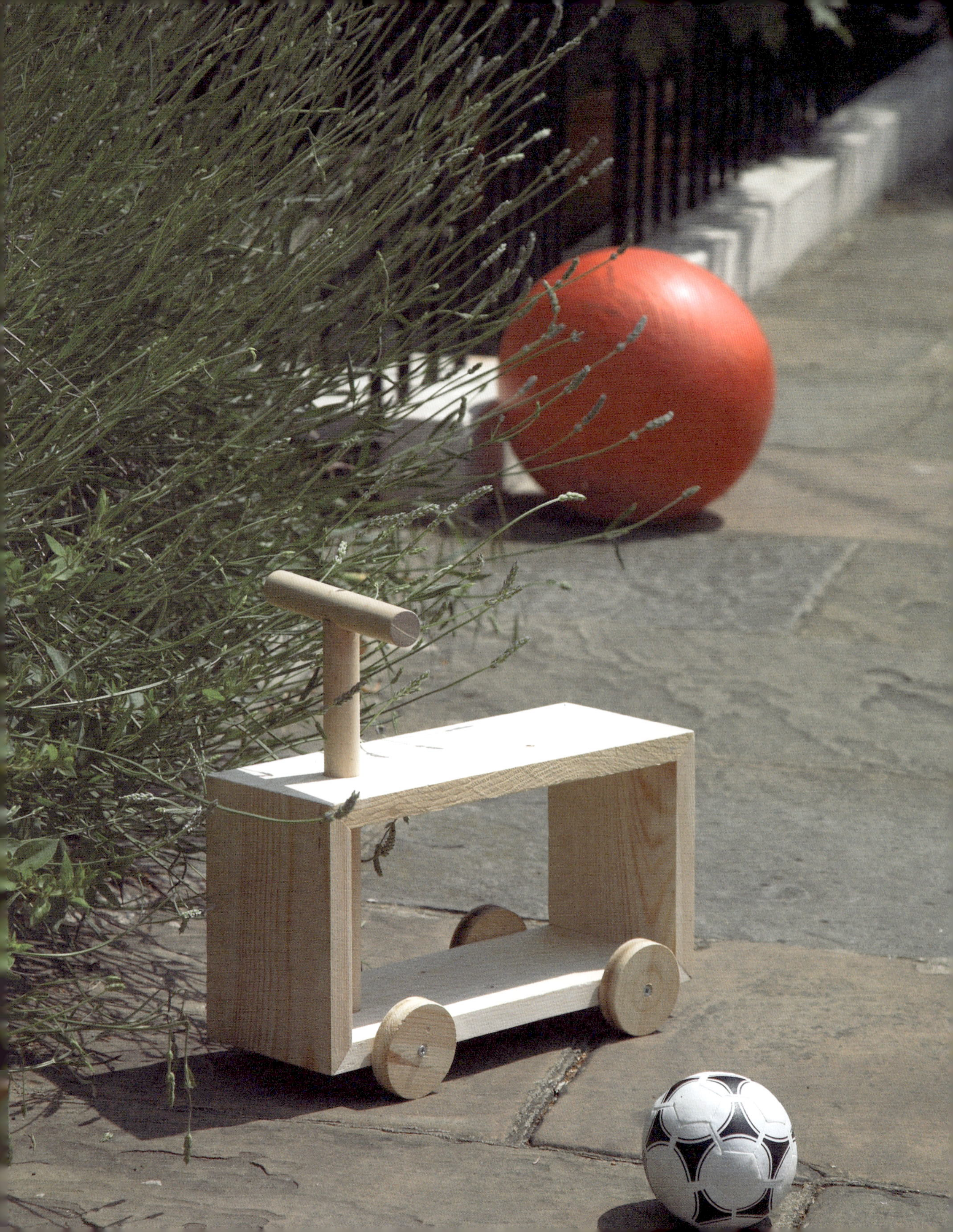

Trundle Scooter

The starting point for this child's scooter was a simple, strong frame construction. I have made the wheels out of offcuts, but you could use small rubber wheels instead. It can be fun to make this with your child, but if he or she is a bit young to participate in the woodwork, you could perhaps paint it together to give the scooter a personalized appearance.

Instructions

WHAT YOU NEED

Wood
Plank: 1200 x 145 x 20mm (3ft 11 1/2in x 6in x 1in) (scooter)
Offcut: 200 x 200 x18mm (8 x 8 x 1in) (wheels)
Dowelling: 520 x 27mm in diameter (1ft 9in x 1in) (handlebar)
Screws: 4 part-threaded - no thread in the top 15mm (5/8in), 4mm gauge x 70mm long (size 8, 2 5/8in) (wheels)
Screws: 2, 4mm gauge x 70mm long (size 8, 2 3/4in) (handlebar)
Washers: 4
Wood glue
Sandpaper

Saw and mitre box, or electric saw that can cut angles
Drill
Flat drill bit: 28mm; multi-purpose twist bit: 3mm
Holesaw: 70mm

Pilot-countersink bit: 4mm
Half-round wood file
Band clamp (ratchet strap and plastic corner protectors)
Screwdriver

TECHNIQUES

Measuring and marking: see page 86
Sawing wood: see pages 86-7, 92
Planing and sanding: see pages 87, 92
Drilling holes: see pages 88-9, 92
Gluing and clamping: see pages 93 and 90
Finishes for wood: see page 91
Mitred joints: see page 93

FRONT VIEW

190mm
Handlebar
Handlebar upright
Front

SIDE VIEW

400mm
Seat
Back
200mm
Wheelbase

VIEW FROM ABOVE

Handlebar
Seat
Wheel

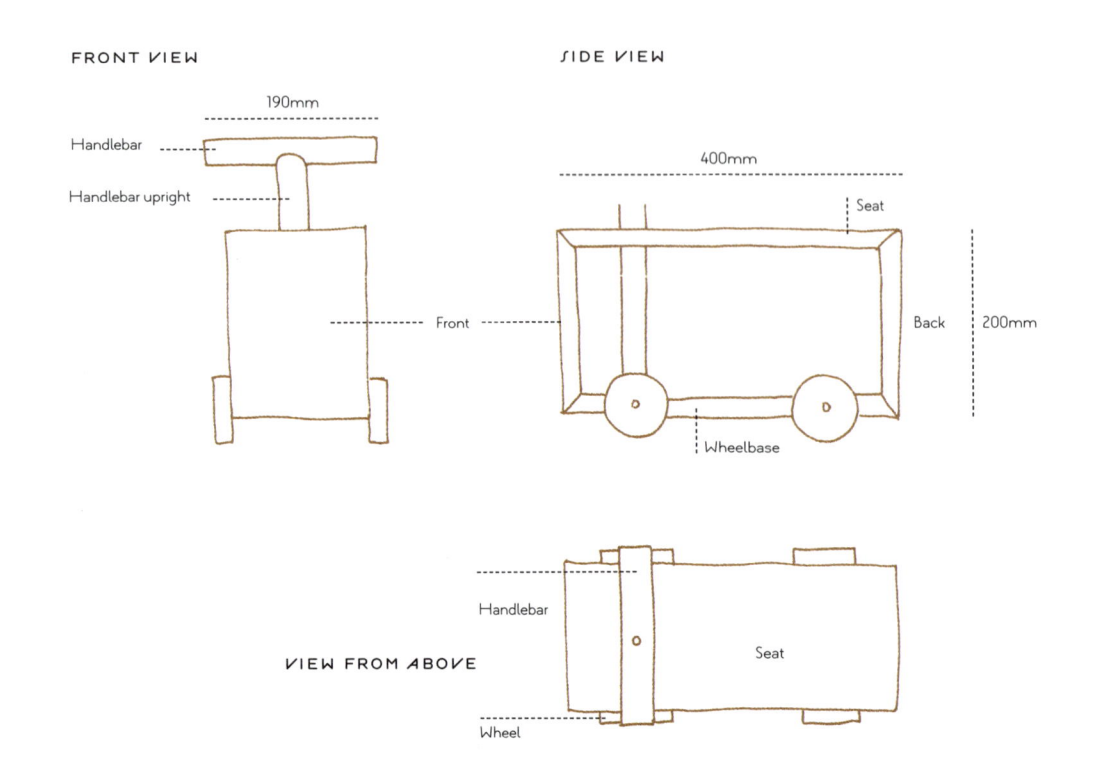

68 One Piece of Wood

1

Cut the wood for the frame: two lengths of 400mm (1ft 4in) for the seat and wheelbase, and two lengths of 200mm (8in) for the front and back end. Mitre the short end of each piece at a 45° angle, so the four parts will come together as a frame (see page 93).

2

With the top side of the seat board upwards, drill a hole for the upright part of the handlebar with the 28mm drill bit, positioning the centre of the hole 94mm (3¾in) from the short end and centring it. The diameter of the hole is 1mm (1/32in) bigger than the handlebar upright.

On the top side of the wheelbase (which will become the inside of the frame), drill a matching hole to a depth of about 10mm (3/8in). Centre it 74mm (3in) from the short edge. Place the pieces of the frame together for a test fit.

3

Glue the four parts of the frame together. Use a ratchet strap and corner protectors to hold it securely until the glue has set.

Trundle Scooter

Instructions

4

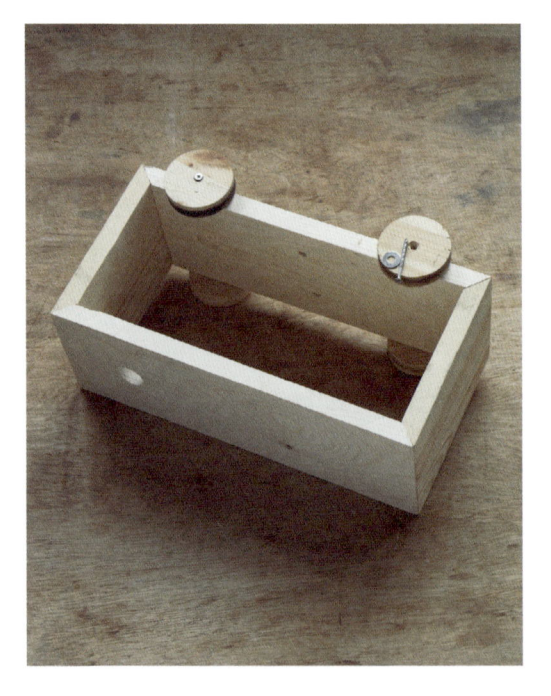

Clamp the offcut to the worktable and cut out the wheels with the holesaw. This will automatically drill a hole in the centre of the wheel at the same time.

5

Using the 3mm drill bit, drill a pilot hole for the screws in the side of the wheelbase, 94mm (3³⁄₄in) from the longer, unmitred edge. Screw on the wheels, putting a washer between the frame and the wheel. Do not screw on too tightly – the wheels must run easily.

6

Cut the dowelling into two pieces: 190mm (7^1/$_2$in) long for the handlebar and 330mm (1ft 1in) long for the handlebar upright. File the upright piece on one end so the handlebar can nestle in it.

Drill a pilot hole in the centre of the handlebar and in each end of the upright with the 3mm drill bit. Put a bit of glue on the end of the upright and screw on the handlebar.

7

Push the upright through the hole in the seat and locate the end in the hole in the wheelbase. Use the file to enlarge the hole if necessary.

On the underside of the wheelbase, locate the position of the upright by measuring as in step 2. Drill a pilot hole with the 3mm drill bit, then insert a screw through the wheelbase and into the upright. Give all the parts a light sanding. That's it: it's ready to ride.

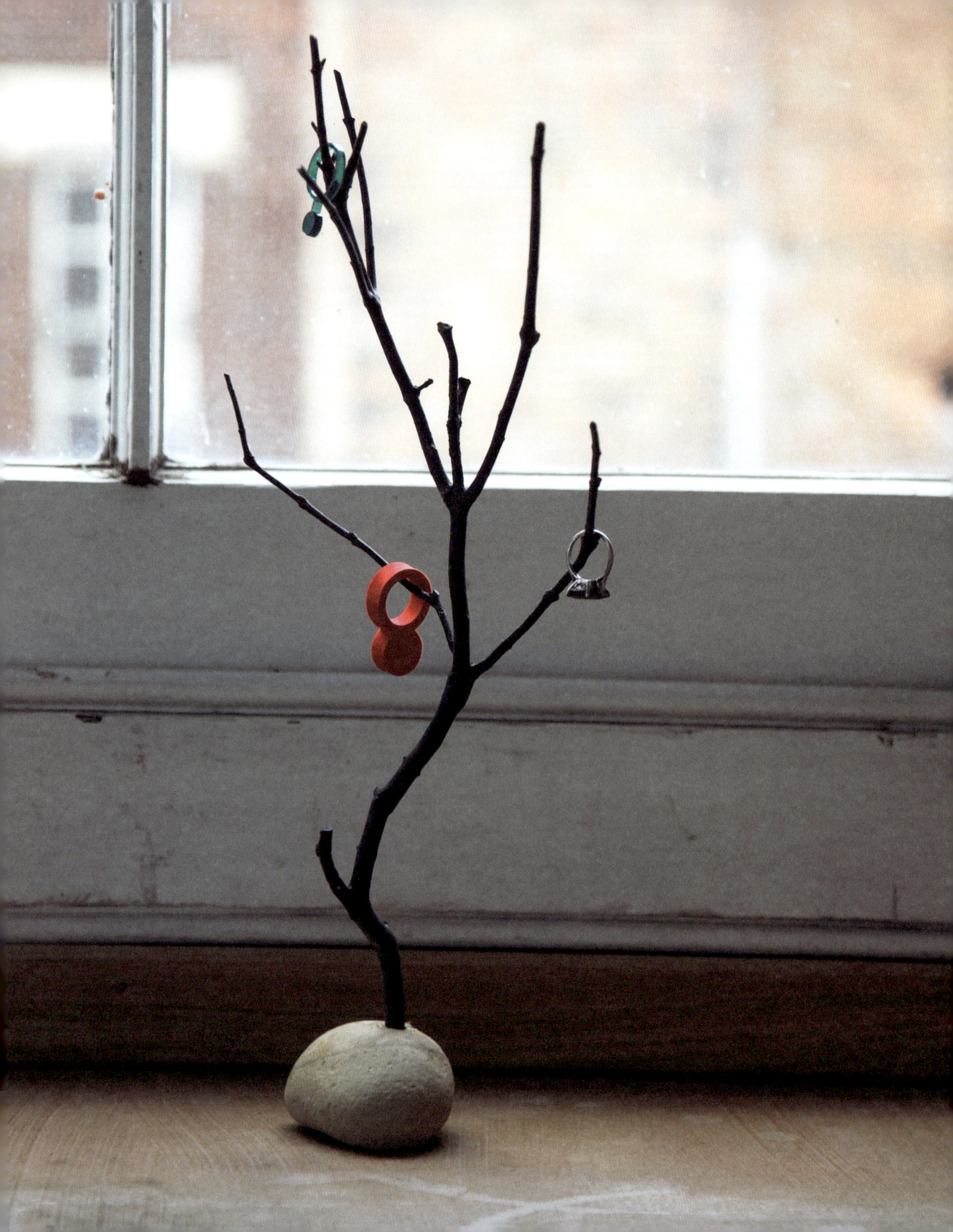

Jewellery Tree

The idea of this jewellery tree was to contrast the beautiful simplicity of a twig with the sophistication of a piece of jewellery. Most of the pieces of jewellery I own are gifts or things I have bought when travelling, so they all hold special memories. I like to look at them when they're not being worn, too – in the same way that I look at pictures on display. As well as being functional, the jewellery tree also becomes an object that is decorative in its own right. The base can be made from a pebble or a block of wood.

Instructions

WHAT YOU NEED

Nice little twig with branches that are evenly distributed
Base: soft stone (limestone) or a square block of wood
Spray paint
Wood glue

Drill
Masonry drill bit: diameter to match that of branch
Saw

TECHNIQUES

Drilling holes: see pages 88–9, 92
Finishes for wood: see page 91

1

Make the base (I made two trees, one with a stone base and one with a wooden base). Drill a hole in the centre of the top of the stone or block of wood. The wooden block I used measured 60 x 60 x 60mm (2³⁄₈ x 2³⁄₈ x 2³⁄₈in).

2

Spray the twig with paint and leave to dry. The block can be left unpainted or painted it in a colour of your choice; I sprayed it black, but gold would look good.

3

Put a bit of glue in the hole and insert the twig, making sure it stands straight. Leave to dry, then dress the tree by draping it in your favourite pieces of jewellery.

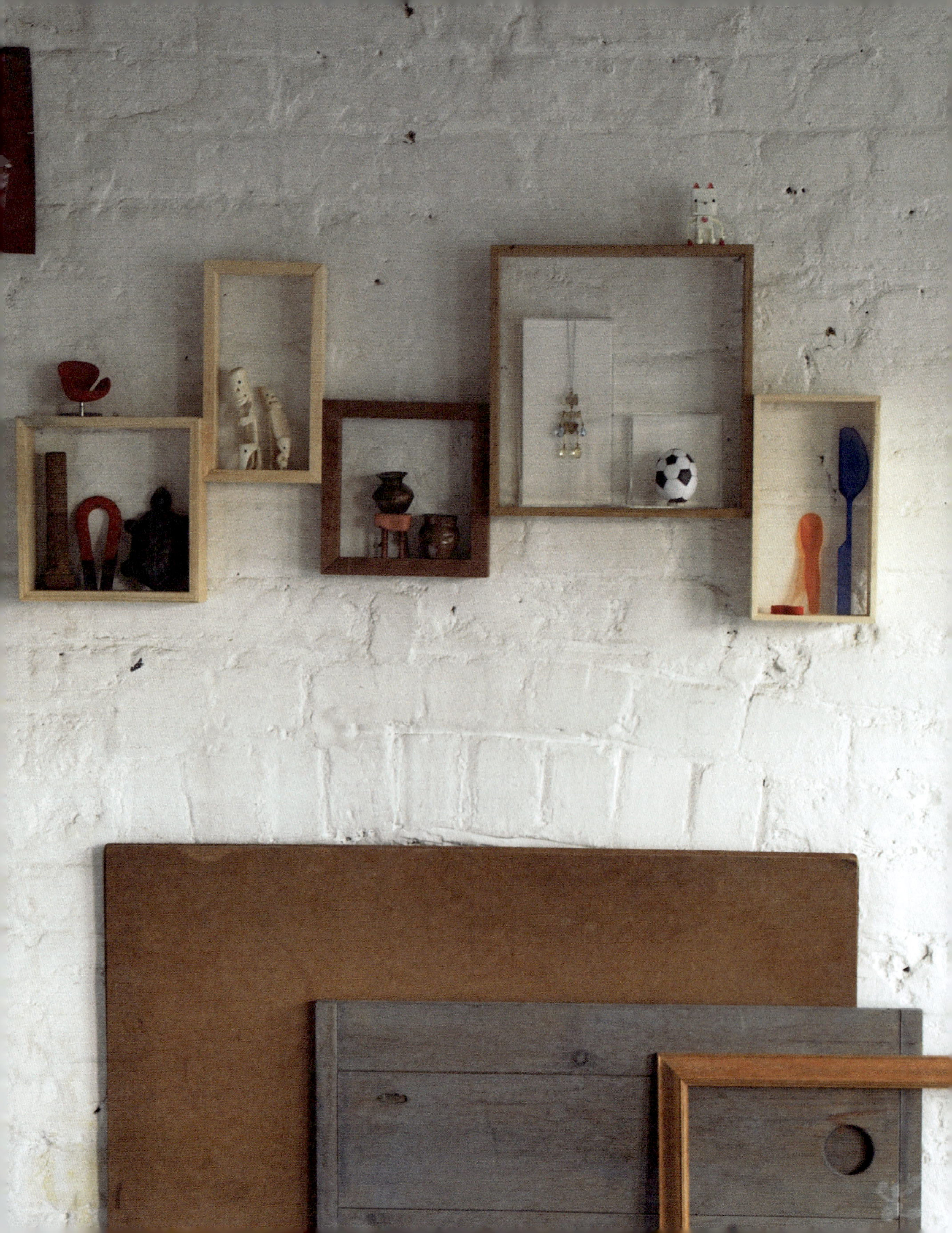

Wonder Frames

With this system of frames, you can create your own *wunderkammer* (chamber of wonders). A collection of objects, souvenirs and images can be organized and displayed in an appealing way. It is always nice to frame things – it makes them look more appreciated. I have made a handful of frames, all with different dimensions in the wood and frame size. Make as many or as few as you wish, or add frames in the future. You can design the frames to fit a specific space or hang them in a random pattern. It is a decorative way to order and display things that are meaningful to you. I have made five frames out of the sections of wood described here, but you can make them to other sizes as you wish.

Instructions

WHAT YOU NEED

Wood: selection of planks
- 760 x 70 x 8mm (2ft 6in x 2$^{3}/_{4}$in x $^{1}/_{4}$in) (frame 1)
- 730 x 42 x 12mm (2ft 4$^{3}/_{4}$in x 1$^{3}/_{4}$in x $^{1}/_{2}$in) (frame 2)
- 1150 x 50 x 10mm (3ft 9$^{1}/_{4}$in x 2in x $^{1}/_{4}$in) (frame 3)
- 750 x 33 x 18mm (2ft 5$^{1}/_{2}$in x 1$^{1}/_{2}$in x $^{3}/_{4}$in) (frame 4)
- 810 x 60 x 10mm (2ft 7$^{7}/_{8}$in x 2$^{1}/_{2}$in x $^{1}/_{4}$in) (frame 5)

Wood glue
Frame hangers or mirror plates with screws: 2 minimum (depends on total number of frames)

Saw and mitre box, or electric saw that can cut angles
Clamps
Band clamps (ratchet straps and plastic corner protectors)

TECHNIQUES

Measuring and marking: see page 86
Sawing wood: see pages 86–7, 92
Planing and sanding: see pages 87, 92
Drilling holes: see pages 88–9, 92
Gluing and clamping: see pages 93 and 90
Mitred joints: see page 93

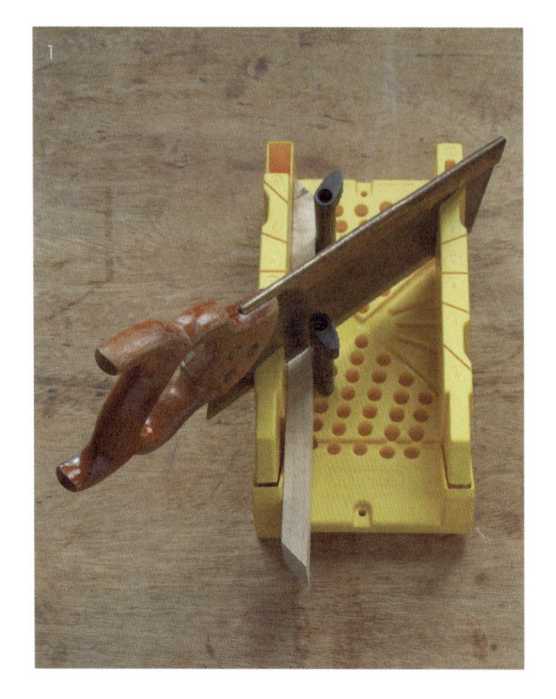

1

Cut the wood to size to make five frames – see frame dimensions below. Mitre the short ends (see page 93).
Frames 1 and 2: 240 x 135mm (9 x 6in)
Frame 3: 285 x 285mm (11$^{1}/_{4}$ x 11$^{1}/_{4}$in)
Frame 4: 185 x 185mm (7$^{1}/_{4}$ x 7$^{1}/_{4}$in)
Frame 5: 200 x 200mm (7$^{7}/_{8}$ x 7$^{7}/_{8}$in)

2

Glue the four sides of each frame together. Use a strap and corner protectors to hold the pieces in the correct position while the frame dries.

3

Lay out the frames in a configuration that you like and glue them together one by one. Use clamps to hold the row of frames together until the glue has dried. The glue should be sufficient to hold small frames that are not going to carry much weight, but if you are making bigger frames that will carry heavier items, you need to screw them together as well as glue them.

4

Fix the frame hangers/mirror plates to the back of the row of frames. The frame should cover most of the hanger. A single hanger at each end of the row of frames should be sufficient unless you plan to display heavy items. Hang the row of frames on the wall.

Different frame configurations

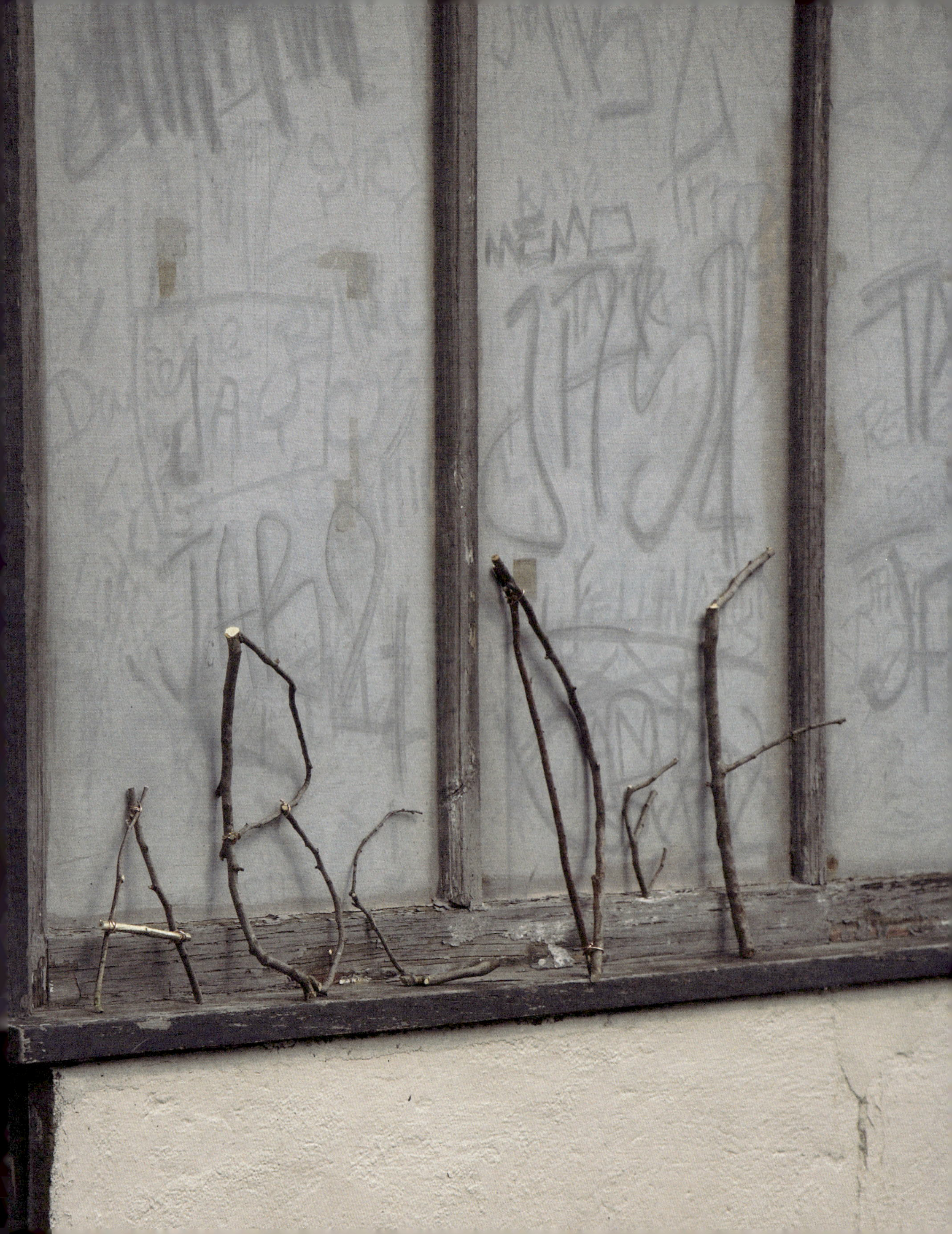
MEMO
ABCDEF

Twig Alphabet

This is a fun and charming way to make signs, or children's names to hang on their bedroom door. You can make the letters individually, or merge letters together as a logotype. You will need a huge pile of twigs: find someone who has been pruning shrubs – autumn is a good time for this. Lay out the twigs on the ground and pick out the ones with shapes that look most suitable for the letters you have in mind.

Instructions

WHAT YOU NEED

Twigs
Water
Roll of string

Strong, sharp scissors or pruning scissors

1
Decide which letters you need (I decided to make the alphabet). The letters can be formed in many different ways, and it is best to inspect the shapes of the twigs that you have collected and pick the ones that have some curves or bends that work with the letter you are trying to make. Some letters can be made out of one twig; other letters require several twigs to be tied together.

2

Choose the twigs for each letter and start construction, tying them together with string. When you need to bend a twig to form a shape, dampen it and bend it gently so that it does not break. If the twig can't be bent to shape in one go, do it in stages – tie the ends together with string and leave for some hours, and then squeeze them a bit more. You can do this several times as the wood slowly softens up.

3

Continue making the letters – forming them in the most appropriate way according to the twigs you have. As an alternative binding material, you could use copper wire.

4

Display the letters by hanging them on a small nail in the wall or hook in a door, or suspend from a hook in the ceiling.

Twig Alphabet

Tools & Equipment

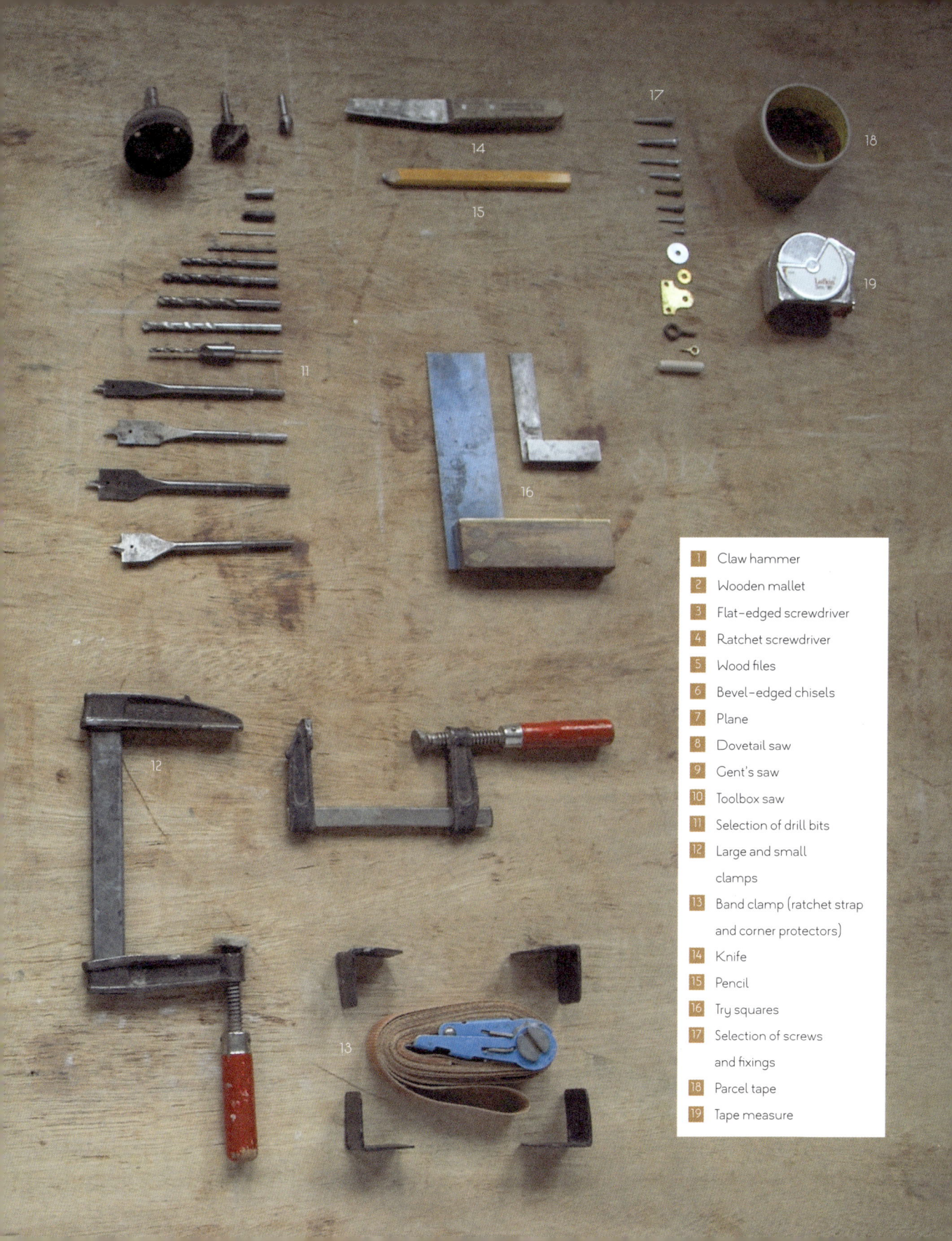

1	Claw hammer
2	Wooden mallet
3	Flat-edged screwdriver
4	Ratchet screwdriver
5	Wood files
6	Bevel-edged chisels
7	Plane
8	Dovetail saw
9	Gent's saw
10	Toolbox saw
11	Selection of drill bits
12	Large and small clamps
13	Band clamp (ratchet strap and corner protectors)
14	Knife
15	Pencil
16	Try squares
17	Selection of screws and fixings
18	Parcel tape
19	Tape measure

Tools & Equipment

To make the projects in this book, you need only a basic range of tools: ruler, tape measure, try square, saw, plane, file, hammer, screwdriver, chisel, drill with a selection of drill bits, a mitre box, sandpaper and wood glue. You'll also need a workbench or a good, solid work table.

HEALTH AND SAFETY

Take appropriate safety precautions: wear safety glasses to protect your eyes from chips of wood that may fly off, and use a dust mask to stop yourself inhaling dust while sawing and sanding. Use power tools with great care, always following the manufacturer's instructions, and make sure that you tie back long hair, and do not wear any dangling jewellery or have sleeves that may get caught up in machinery. If your children are helping with projects, they must be closely supervised at all times.

YOUR WORKING AREA

If possible, set up a permanent workspace where you can keep all your equipment and tools. It needs to be well lit, with enough space to move around easily. You have to be able to ventilate it – with a window or door – for when you are creating a lot of dust, or when you need to allow paint or glue fumes to escape. You need some sort of sturdy worksurface – there are many designs available, from inexpensive folding workbenches to various wooden workbenches suitable for light- and heavy-duty work, incorporating vices and storage space.

MEASURING AND MARKING

Measuring, marking and squaring are, in many ways, the most important aspect of woodworking. If measurements are not exact, the components will not fit together well. A metal tape measure is adequate for taking most measurements. For very accurate dimensions, use a good-quality boxwood rule for long lengths and a steel rule for short lengths. Use a sharp, fine pencil for most marking tasks but a marking knife when extremely precise marking is required. A marking knife is particularly useful for marking chisel lines, because the score in the wood serves as an accurate guide for placing the chisel blade.

A try square is used to draw square lines across boards, to transfer lines from one face to another, and to check the squareness of saw cuts and of planed surfaces.

SAWS

Sawing is the most basic operation involved in making any object in wood, as you must cut the components to size before putting them together. Hand-saws are indispensable, even though an electrical saw may do the job much more quickly. Different types of hand-saw vary in the number of teeth or 'points' per 25mm (1in) they have, and the more a saw has, the finer the cut it will make. A large ripsaw, for example, may have only six points per 25mm, whereas a backsaw can have as many as twenty-two.

Hand-saws are divided into three main types:
- Large saws such as rip, crosscut and panel saws. These are used for rough work. The ripsaw is used for cutting along the grain (called 'ripping'). The crosscut saw has smaller teeth and is for cutting wood across the run of the grain. The panel saw is a smaller crosscut saw with teeth fine enough to give a fairly smooth cut. A toolbox saw is a small crosscut saw.
- Backsaws, such as the tenon saw. These small-toothed crosscut saws are used for fine work. The blade is stiffened across the top with a rib or 'back' of steel or brass. The tenon saw, which is about the most useful of all the hand-saws, is used for most fine crosscuts such as cutting joints.
- Fine saws with narrow, replaceable blades – such as bow, keyhole, coping and fretsaws. These are used for cutting curves.

A pullsaw cuts on the pull stroke only. It is good for sawing in places that are difficult to access, giving you good control and a fine finish. There are several purpose-made hand-saws for cutting irregular shapes in wood.

To cut angles in wood, you will need a mitre box (which is inexpensive to buy). This is an open box with slots on the top at 45° and 90° angles. You insert the piece of wood, and then saw it through the slot.

Eventually, you may wish to invest in an electric saw. If you do a lot of work that requires irregular cuts, an electric jigsaw will cut easily through solid wood as well as sheets of plywood. Bandsaws are available as a small, bench-top machine. These have a blade that runs in a loop, and are good for cutting curved pieces. A compound mitre saw can cut angles with its disc-shaped blade; it is more precise than a mitre box and better for cutting big pieces of wood. A bench table saw has a disc blade set in the centre of a table. It can be used to cut pieces to width and length, or to cut grooves and mitres.

PLANES

To give wood a smooth finish, use a hand plane. These are available in different lengths and types. A smoothing plane is the last plane used on a surface to create a very smooth finish; it can also be used for planing edges and levelling boards. A block plane is designed to plane end grain (the end of a board or section); it is also used for chamfering (angling square edges) and finishing joints.

SANDPAPER

Sanding involves the use of a series of abrasive papers, from coarse to fine, to achieve the smoothest possible finish. There are different types of abrasive paper, coated with crushed glass, sand, aluminium oxide or garnet. Many woodworkers prefer garnet paper because it is harder than glasspaper or sandpaper and therefore cuts more quickly and cleanly. Abrasives are graded from rough to smooth by grit size: the higher the number, the finer the abrasive. For a rough, open-grained wood such as oak, you may have to start sanding with 80-grit, but birch plywood is already quite smooth and so 150- or 240-grit will be more suitable.

FILES AND CHISELS

Bevel-edged chisels are used to cut out areas of wood: you hold the chisel in one hand and hit it with a mallet. It is useful to have a range of these chisels in different sizes.

Metal files are used to file down areas of wood, and they are available in flat or rounded versions. A half-round file can be used to file the edges of a hole to a nice rounded finish.

HAMMERS

Although a hammer is rarely needed in the projects, this is a basic toolbox item. For general work, a claw hammer is good for bashing in nails or removing them with the claw-shaped end. A pin hammer is smaller and lighter, and suitable for tapping in small nails and pins. A rubber mallet is ideal for more delicate tasks, such as gently knocking in dowel pegs.

SCREWDRIVERS

The range of screwdrivers you need depends on the type of screws you intend to use. For slot-headed screws you need a flat screwdriver; for cross-headed screws such as Phillips or Pozidrive, you need a screwdriver designed especially for them. A cordless drill-driver is a very useful item: with a screwdriver bit inserted, it can be used to drive in screws quickly, and is great if you have a lot to insert.

KNIVES

A multi-purpose craft knife or Stanley knife comes in handy for a range of marking and cutting tasks, as does a sharp pair of strong, ordinary scissors.

DRILL AND DRILL BITS

A drill is a tool fitted with any of various drill bits and used to bore holes. Drill bits are available in standard sizes; in this book they are listed in millimetres (diameter), but you can find a comprehensive chart listing metric drill sizes and imperial equivalents, together with the relevant screw sizes, online at the website for www.lincolnmachine.com. Click 'Technical Information' and then 'Tap Drill Chart'.

To drill a satisfactory hole in any material, the correct type of drill bit must be used. For basic requirements, a set of multi-purpose high-speed steel (HSS) twist drill bits and some

Tools & Equipment

masonry bits will probably be sufficient for the average handyman or woman. But for more sophisticated jobs and materials, other bits will be required – perhaps larger, or designed for a specific material or purpose. Good-quality drill bits can be expensive, so take care of them by keeping them in a case or box, rather than allowing them to roll around loose in a toolbox, where the cutting edges may become damaged.

Twist bits are probably the most common type of drill bit. The front edges cut the material and the spirals along the length remove the debris from the hole. They can be used on timber, metal, plastics and similar materials. Most twist bits are made from either high-speed steel (HSS) or carbon steel.

- → High-speed steel (HSS) bits are suitable for drilling most types of material; when drilling metal, they stand up to the high temperatures generated.
- → Carbon steel bits are specially ground for drilling wood and should not be used for drilling metal. They tend to be more brittle and less flexible than HSS bits.

Twist drills are usually available in sizes from 0.8mm to larger than 12mm. They are designed for drilling relatively small holes, and sometimes tend to clog quickly, especially when the wood is green (unseasoned). So, when drilling deep holes (especially in hardwood), the bit should be withdrawn regularly to remove the waste. Special care is required when using the smallest sizes of bit, since these are thin and brittle. Always hold the drill square to the work and apply only light pressure when drilling.

Masonry bits are, as the name suggests, designed for drilling into brick, block, stone, quarry tiles or concrete. The cutting tip is often made from tungsten carbide bonded to a spiralled steel shaft. Most masonry bits can be used with a hammer-action power drill. Always use a slow rotational speed for drilling into these materials to prevent the tip overheating, and withdraw the bit frequently to remove dust.

A pilot drill bit is used to drill a pilot hole – a small hole made to give a screw something to bite into. It is usually not necessary when working in soft wood; use pilot holes only when you need to ensure that a screw goes into an exact position, when working into end grain, near the end or edge of the piece of wood, or when using brass screws, which snap easily.

A countersink bit, although not a true 'drill', is used in a power or hand drill to form a conical recess for the head of a countersunk screw to slip into, leaving it flush with the surface of the wood. These bits tend to be designed for use on soft materials such as timber and plastics, not metals. When used with a power drill to countersink an existing hole, the bit may 'chatter', leaving a rough surface. Better results will be obtained if the countersink bit is used before the hole is drilled, and then take care to ensure that the hole is in the centre of the countersunk depression. There are also combination countersink drills: a clearance-countersink bit drills a hole and makes a countersunk depression at the same time, and a pilot-countersink bit drills a pilot hole and countersinks it all in one stroke.

Flat wood bits are intended for power drill use only. The centre point locates the bit and the flat steel on either side cuts away the timber. These bits are used to drill fairly large, flat-bottomed holes (with a central point). The larger bits require a fairly powerful drill in order to bore deep holes. Flat wood bits cause a lot of splintering as they break out of the back of the

Tools & Equipment

workpiece – use a sacrificial backing board to reduce this. This type of bit is not really suitable for enlarging an existing hole. Sizes range between 8–32mm.

A holesaw is used for cutting large, fixed-diameter holes in wood or plastic. They will usually cut to a depth of up to 18mm (¹¹/₁₆in), although deeper-cutting versions are available. Use the power drill at a low speed as the holesaw cuts its way through the material.

A Forstner bit is used to form holes with a flat bottom, such as those needed for kitchen cupboard hinges. It is best to fix the power drill into a drill stand to use it, as there's little in the way of a central point. If used freehand, the positioning is difficult to control.

CLAMPS

Clamps are essential, even for the smallest woodworking job. They not only hold wood together tightly while the glue sets to form a permanent bond, but are frequently used to hold pieces when you need to have both hands free to work. They are also useful during assembly, to pull and hold joints together and to straighten out framework constructions. There are many special clamps for specific jobs, for example mitre clamps, which are used to hold mitred pieces. I also use a band clamp (ratchet strap and plastic corner protectors), for example in the Trundle Scooter project on page 66, to hold a frame together while the glue dries. The strap is placed around the frame, over the corner protectors, and then tightened to hold everything together securely. Check for squareness before leaving items such as this to dry. This way of clamping is also useful for gluing awkwardly shaped objects together.

SCREWS

Use single-thread woodscrews (the thread is the spiral shape along the length of the screw). Screw sizes can be confusing, as they are sometimes described in metric and sometimes in imperial. Screw size is measured by the diameter of the screw's shank (gauge), and the length from its head to the point of the screw.

Screws have different 'drive recesses' – the part of the head in which you place the driver bit or screwdriver in order to drive in the screw. The slotted screwhead has a simple slot and requires a flat-headed screwdriver. Cross-headed screws, such as Philips or Pozidrive, feature a cross and require a special matching screwdriver to fit them.

The screwheads also come in different shapes. They may be flat or domed; countersink screws have angled heads to allow them to lie flush with or just below the surface when screwed in. You can get self-countersink screws that penetrate the wood without requiring you to drill a hole with a pilot-countersink drill bit. These screws are more expensive, come in a smaller range of sizes and are less available.

Part-threaded screws have a thread that runs only part of the way along the shaft. These screws are useful for situations where you want to allow a joined part to move, for example the

'SCREW SIZE IS MEASURED BY THE DIAMETER OF THE SCREW'S SHANK (GAUGE), AND THE LENGTH FROM ITS HEAD TO THE POINT OF THE SCREW.'

limbs of the Blackboard Robot (see page 28), or the wheels on the Trundle Scooter (see page 66).

GLUE

There are many special glues available for gluing wood. Choose the right glue for the job depending on the strength, resistance to wear and water, and gap-filling properties that you require. The ability of a glue to fill gaps becomes important when making joints, as the pieces being joined may not be a perfect fit and the glue fills in the connection. Two main types of adhesive are used: PVA white woodworking glue, available in plastic squeezy bottles for general work, and syntactic resin glue for work that has to be waterproof.

SUNDRIES

Even items of stationery are useful for woodwork! Masking tape is used to mask off areas that you want to keep paint-free whilst applying paint; parcel tape can be used to hold lightweight items together while they dry, instead of a clamp – as in, for example, the plywood Herb Carrier on page 46.

FINISHES FOR WOOD

Wood doesn't necessarily have to have a finish applied to it. So long as the piece is kept in a dry environment, any marks can be removed by rubbing with steel wool or very fine sandpaper. Finishes are applied to seal the surface of wood and protect it from moisture, which causes the wood to warp and creates unsightly stains. If the wood is attractively grained, the finish should enhance the pattern. Finishes include oil, wax, shellac, lacquer or paint. Items that will remain outdoors can be protected with a preservative paint or stain: those available include varieties that are friendly to people, animals and plants.

I have used special paint for the Blackboard Robot on page 28, which coats the surface to give it the quality of a blackboard. All household paints designed for wood are suitable for the projects. I have used spray paint for the Jewellery Trees on page 72; always wear a mask when applying it. Use paints in a well-ventilated area.

DOWEL PEGS

Wooden dowel pegs are used in dowelled joints to join together two components. A dowel is glued into a hole in one piece, and then inserted into a hole in the corresponding piece. You can buy a dowel jig kit to help you standardize the location of the holes on components, but it is also possible to make your own (see page 93).

Techniques

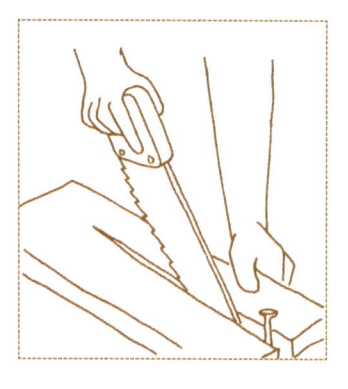

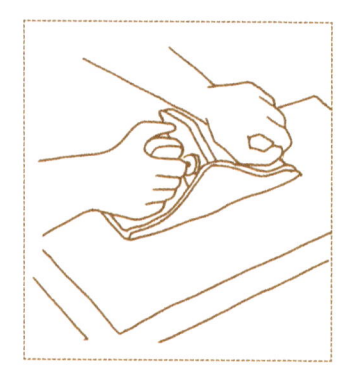

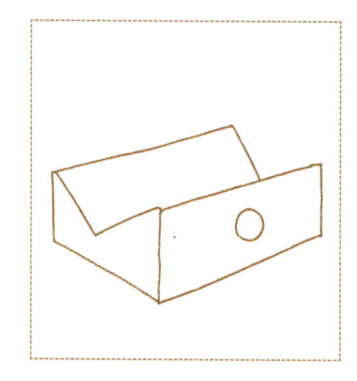

SAWING

When sawing with a hand-saw, hold the handle with the index finger pointing along the blade for better control. Using your thumb as a guide, start the saw cut at a low angle, then raise the saw to about 45°. The work should always be well supported on trestles, clamped to the bench or held in a vice. During ripping, some boards have a tendency to spring together as you cut, jamming the saw blade. The easiest way to remedy this is to place a short wedge or a nail in the cut to keep the edges apart. When crosscutting, it is important to prevent the end from splitting off before you have finished the cut – you can support both sides of the cut, as you finish the cut, with masking tape.

PLANING

When planing, make sure the board is held on a firm, horizontal surface. The longer the plane, the more accurate the results. Work with a smooth motion, applying even pressure along the whole length (see centre illustration above). Assess the work for straightness frequently by sighting along the length, and check for squareness by using a try square.

SANDING

To sand, make sure the work is held firmly on the workbench or in a vice, wrap the abrasive paper around a sanding block and sand with even strokes, working with the grain.

DRILLING

Making and using a depth stop
If you want to ensure that you drill consistently to a certain depth, put a small piece of masking tape around the drill at the required depth. As you drill, you will be able to see when the drill has penetrated the wood as far as you want it to go.

Drilling at an angle
To drill at an angle, clamp the wood securely. Hold the drill at a suitable angle and drill the hole. For projects such as the 'Nose' Hooks (see page 18), the angle does not need to be precise. If you want a 45° hole, make a jig (see illustration above right; also page 93). Cut the jig according to the angles shown (45°) and drill a hole straight through the side. Put the project piece in the jig and drill through the hole in the jig to produce a 45° hole.

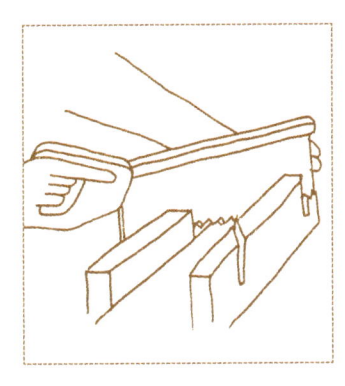

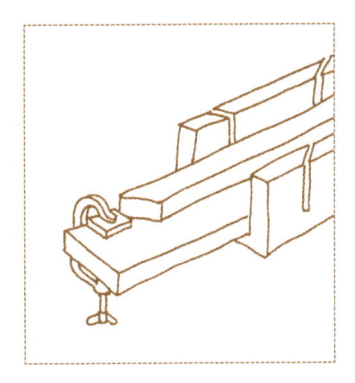

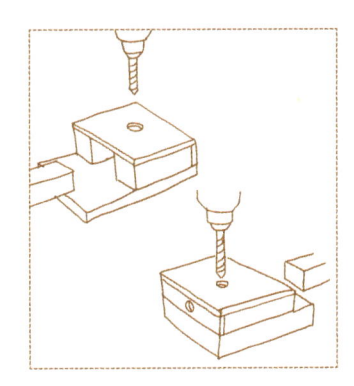

GLUING

When gluing, make sure the surfaces are straight and free from dirt, dust and oil. When making joints, test for fit before gluing. Spread adhesive evenly on the joint with a stick or glue spreader. Bring the joint together and then clamp it. Do not clamp it so tightly that all the glue is squeezed out. Check that the work is held correctly, that frames are square, surfaces are straight and joints are flush. Clean off excess glue on the workpiece and from worksurfaces.

FORMING JOINTS

Mitred joint

The mitred joint is used to connect two pieces at right angles. Each piece is cut to 45°, so that when they are fitted together, they form a 90° corner. Mitres can also be cut at other angles. Mitred joints are most often used to connect mouldings or frames.

To cut pieces of wood at an accurate 45° angle, use a tenon saw and a mitre box. Place the piece to be cut in the box and saw with light, even strokes through the slots in the mitre box (pictured top left). Then turn the piece around to cut the other end. Remember to cut the angles in opposite directions.

To make a frame, you need to cut mitres on the ends of all four pieces. Remember that the opposite sides of the frame must be identical in length for the joint to close properly. To cut a second piece to match the length of the first, clamp a block to the base as a guide (pictured centre).

Dowelled joint

A dowelled joint is one in which the two pieces are joined at right angles, using dowel pegs that are located in one piece and fit into holes in the corresponding piece. It is important that the holes are drilled precisely and match up with the dowel pegs perfectly. You can buy standard wooden dowel pegs, which are 30mm (1¼in) long and 6mm (¼in) in diameter.

The dowelled joint is used a lot when making furniture. It is a perfect joint for making in the home workshop as it requires little equipment and is quite easy to do. I have used it for the Elegant Trestle (see page 42). It is best to make a jig to make sure that the dowel holes match up.

Cut a piece of wood to the same dimensions as the project pieces and drill a hole in the relevant places to centre the holes the set distance from the edge of the wood. Clamp the jig on the project piece and drill through the holes into the wood below (pictured top right).

Techniques

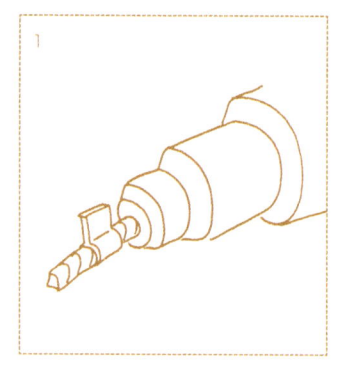

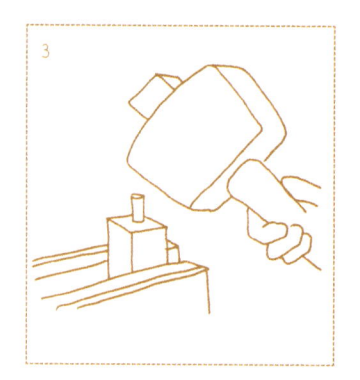

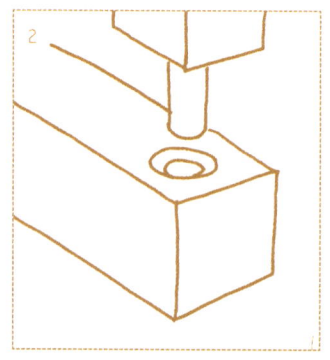

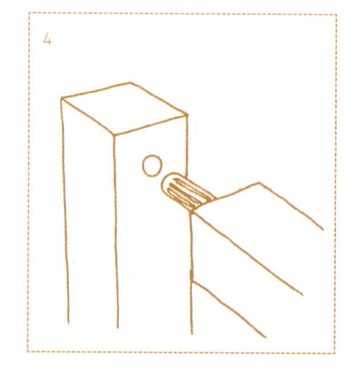

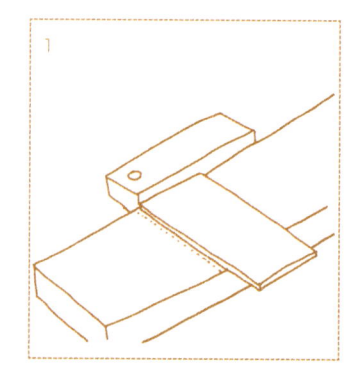

MAKING A DOWELLED JOINT

1 Use a home-made depth stop (see Drilling, page 92) to drill the holes to the correct depth. Drill the holes just slightly deeper then the dowel pegs. The holes should be square to the face of the wood.

2 Countersink the holes a little. This makes it easier to locate the dowel pegs and also collects any overflow of glue.

3 To assemble the joint, the pegs are set in the peg holes first (this pegged piece will then be joined to the other piece). Apply glue to the hole only, to prevent the dowel peg from swelling, and tap the peg in with a mallet, not a hammer. Use light taps so the end of the peg does not split. Allow to dry.

4 Squirt a little glue in the hole of the matching piece, and locate the pegged piece in the hole. Allow to dry.

5 If a hole is out of line, glue a dowel in the faulty hole and cut it off flush, then re-drill a new hole in the correct place.

MAKING A CROSS–HALVING JOINT

In the Pallet Stool (see page 22), the cross shape at the base is made using a cross-halving joint. Halving joints are easy to make. Mark the pieces carefully first.

1 Work on one component at a time. Draw out the position of the joint on the top face of the pieces of wood with a ruler and try square.

2 Continue the parallel lines down each of the side edges.

94 One Piece of Wood

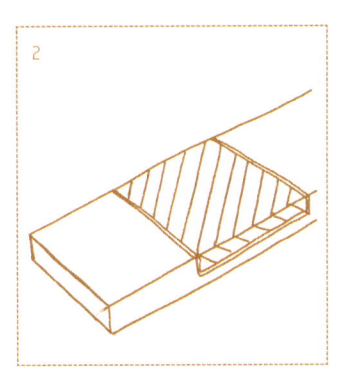

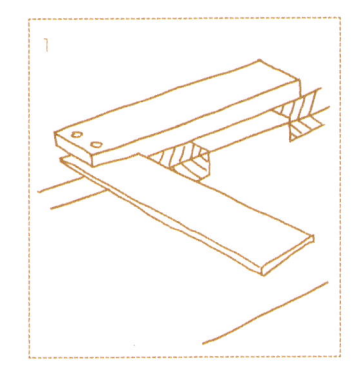

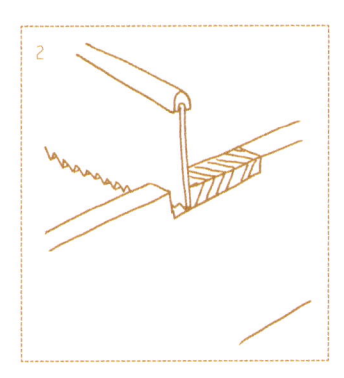

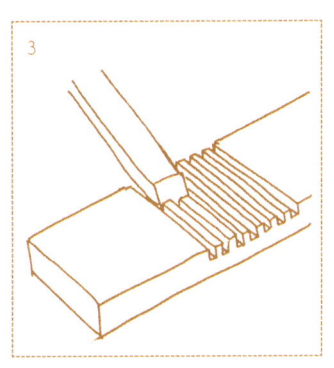

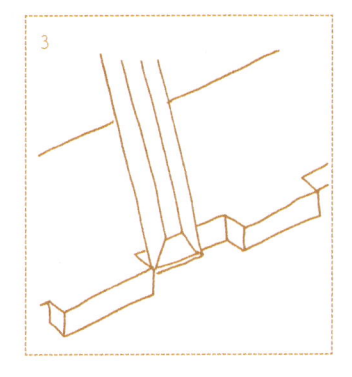

Mark a horizontal line that is half the thickness of the side edge. Shade in the waste area with crossed lines, so it is obvious which part has to be cut away.

3 Cut a series of grooves of equal depth through the waste area, using a tenon saw. Make sure that the cuts stop short of the horizontal line.

4 Use a sharp chisel to chisel out the waste.

5 Test for fit, then glue the joint together. Clamp and leave to dry for 20 minutes.

MAKING A FINGER JOINT

The finger joint can be cut by hand but is most often made by machine. It is also known as a box joint. To make a finger joint by hand, clamp the two pieces together in the vice and mark both pieces across with a try square. You are going to cut one piece with a bit that sticks out, called the pin or finger, and the other piece with a recess for the pin to slot into, called the tail.

1 Clamp both pieces in the vice, butting up against each other. Mark the tail and the pin. Take the wood out of the vice and square the lines down. Before cutting out the waste, mark it with pencil lines, so you do not make a mistake and cut the wrong bit.

2 When cutting the pin, hold the wood vertically in the vice and make sure that you saw on the waste side of the drawn line, otherwise the pin will be too small. After sawing to the line, cut out most of the waste with a small saw. Pare away the final waste with a chisel.

3 Cut out the tail in the same way, with a saw and chisel.

TECHNIQUES 95

RESOURCES

Screwfix
Tools and fixings.
Branches nationwide.
www.screwfix.com

B&Q
Tools, fixings and timber.
Branches nationwide.
www.diy.com

Wickes
Tools, fixings and timber.
Branches nationwide.
www.wickes.co.uk

Homebase
Tools, fixings and timber.
Branches nationwide.
www.homebase.co.uk

Travis Perkins
Tools, fixings and timber.
Branches nationwide.
www.travisperkins.co.uk

Machine Mart
Tools and fixings.
Branches nationwide.
www.machinemart.co.uk

City Wood Company Ltd.
Timber merchant.
Lochnagar Street, Poplar,
London E14 0LA.
Tel: 07867 885 115
Email: info@citywood.co.uk
www.citywood.co.uk

National Community Wood Recycling Project
For information on wood recycling projects nationwide.
7 Gloucester Yard,
121-123 Gloucester Rd.,
Brighton BN1 4AF.
Tel: 01273 600503.
email: info@communitywoodrecycling.org.uk
www.communitywoodrecycling.org.uk/

Cecil W. Tyzack
Specialist tool merchant.
79-81 Kingsland Road
London E2 8AG.
Tel: 020 7739 2630.

ACKNOWLEDGEMENTS

This book has been a lovely opportunity to play around in the workshop. I'm very grateful to Miriam Hyslop, commissioning editor at Collins & Brown, for asking me to write it.

A very special thanks to Loopy - who graciously gives me the benefit of his forty years of woodworking experience and lets me use his wonderful workshop, which is crammed with equipment any carpenter would be envious of. Loopy has also taught me most of what I know about woodworking. He has always got a trick up his sleeve, which he very generously shares with me.

Thanks to my family - who test out my designs, make the whole process fun and tell me 'how it should be'. Especial thanks to my husband Jack Mama, for being the lovely person he is and for always supporting me in my work. My children, Otto Mama and Lula Mama, are an endless source of inspiration and always ready to join in with a saw, hammer and paintbrushes.

I would like to thank the great team at Collins & Brown and designer Nihal Yesil for bringing all the photos, text and drawings together into a lovely book; also the editor, Fiona Corbridge, for patiently making sense of all the fragments of text and weeding out all my mistakes, and Kristin Perers and Alex Lewis for the beautiful photos.